THE MUTINY ON BOARD THE

H.M.S.
BOUNTY

Retold by Kenton K. Smith
Illustrated by Helle Urban

CONTENTS

THE CAPTAIN REMEMBERS. . .

I remember that day . . . I remember it well.

I remember what it was like to awaken in the morning and find myself surrounded by four men. In my mind's eye I can still see the grim, hardened looks on their faces. . . .

I remember being tossed around like a rag doll as my hands were bound behind me, and being dragged onto the deck like a hog ready for slaughter. . . .

I remember that it had the feel of an ordinary day. The good salt air was fresh in my lungs. Above me the morning breezes filled the sails. The sound of waves lapping against the bow of the ship was somehow reassuring. But something was wrong! I was no longer in command, and I did not know what the unsmiling men around me were going to do. . . .

I remember how hope sank within me when I left the ship. But it quickly rose again and was joined by determination. I was going to survive!

And I remember the days that followed. They seem now like a long and horrible nightmare. Once again I can feel my stomach aching from hunger, my body shivering in a never-ending round of wetness and cold, and my mind fighting the temptation to give up.

Yes, I remember, and I want you to share it with me, as I remember it all one more time. . . .

CHAPTER 1

Bligh, The Bounty, and Breadfruit

D o you remember a time when you took on an exciting new task? Perhaps it was a job you had been given or a game you wanted to play well or a subject about which you wished to know more. You may have been a little bit frightened at getting into something new and different, but you were also eager to get started.

If you have had that kind of experience, then you know how I felt that day when I first saw her. She was not the first ship I had commanded, but she was special nevertheless.

I shall admit it: I felt a moment of fright when I viewed her for the first time. She was a mighty ship, but I knew that the sea can often be mightier. How well would she handle the pounding of ocean waters against her sides? What damage might violent, rushing winds do to her masts and rigging and sails? I would soon leave my homeland as her captain, but would I return?

But the fright quickly gave way to eagerness. I wanted to walk her deck and stand in the shadow of her sails. I hungered for the feel of the ocean rolling beneath her hull. And I longed for that moment when I could begin to issue my commands and see them carried out.

She is gone now. I am not able to ride her across the waves. But oh, how well I remember the *Bounty*. . . .

My name is Bligh, William Bligh. That is spelled B-L-I-G-H, not B-L-Y. It rhymes with "sigh," not "brig." I am an Englishman and a man of the sea. I have become well-known as captain of the *Bounty*, and I want to tell you

4

about that ship and its crew. I was the captain of the *H.M.S. Bounty*. The initials "H.M.S." stand for "His Majesty's Ship." In 1787, His Majesty, the King of England, was George the Third. In the summer of that year King George made me captain of the *Bounty* and ordered me to sail to the island of Otaheite in the South Seas to obtain a number of bread-fruit plants. These were to be taken to the West Indies, where breadfruit trees could be grown and could then provide a cheap source of food for slaves working on plantations owned by British planters.

You may already be asking, "What is bread-fruit?" Perhaps you are imagining a fruit shaped like a loaf, with a crusty brown cover. Let me give you a description of the bread-fruit. It is round and grows on a large tree, similar in some ways to an apple tree. Some breadfruits are about the size of a small child's head, and when ripe, they are a soft yel-low color.

You eat the inner part of the fruit. It is as white as snow, and has a slightly sweet taste when eaten raw. Often, however, it is roasted and eaten like bread. Aha, now you know why it is called "breadfruit."

This fruit grows on several islands in the South Seas. But those who planned our mission felt that the ones in Otaheite were the tastiest and also the most likely to survive the passage between the South Seas and the West Indies.

Now, since you are about to take a voyage with me on the *Bounty*, you need to know a little bit about a ship. Try to picture a ship in your mind, or look at a picture of an actual ship such as the *Bounty*, if you have one. What do you see?

Well, first you may see the "hull," which is the ship's body. The hull has a front part and a rear part. We call the front the "bow," and we call the rear the "stern." Imagine yourself standing on the deck. You are likely to know

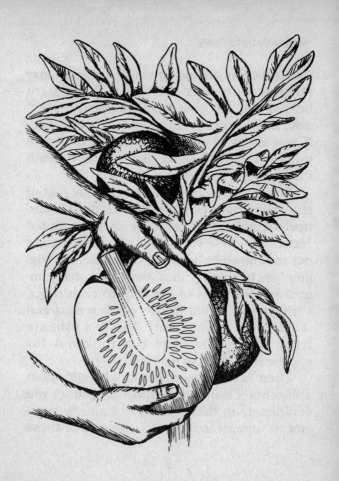

that is the flat surface on which a seaman may stand or walk. Face the bow, with the stern behind you. To your left is the ship's "port" side, and to your right is the "starboard" side. If you are tired of standing on the deck and think you might like to climb down beneath the deck, you "go below."

Before you go below, look up at the part of the ship that rises above the deck. The upright poles that hold the sails are called "masts." The poles that hold the sails straight out are known as "booms" and "gaffs." The "rigging" includes the lines and ropes that connect various parts of the ship to each other. Perhaps you would like to climb a mast and stand in the "crow's nest." That is a platform from which a seaman can look out for approaching ships or for land.

There is much more that can be said about a ship, but it is not my purpose to instruct you completely in these matters. I merely want you to understand, when I use one of these words I have given you. It is my hope that you will be able to picture it in your mind more clearly.

Let me test you on what I have been saying. If I speak of a rope tied to the stern, can you picture that? If I were to write that a man in the crow's nest cried out, "Land, ho! Off the starboard bow!" would you understand what I meant? Of course you would, because I just explained it to you!

But I have been speaking about ships in general. Let me now talk about the *Bounty*. It was on the sixteenth day of August in 1787 that I was appointed to command her. I learned that she was more than ninety feet long, and her width extended to over twenty-four feet. She was capable of carrying as much as 215 tons of cargo.

The ship contained cabins for the surgeon, the gunner, the botanist (of whom I shall have much more to say), and the clerk. These cabins were in the cockpit area, the area from which the vessel is steered. I had a small cabin close by the great cabin. In a moment I shall tell you more about the great cabin. The master's cabin was across from mine. There were berths—that is, places to sleep—nearby for the mates and midshipmen.

The most unusual feature of the ship was the great cabin. It was the place where the breadfruit plants would be kept and cared for. It was constructed with two large skylights,

and on each side there were three openings to provide a flow of air. The floor had been cut full of holes that would hold the pots for the plants. There were pipes set up at the corners of the cabin to carry off the water that drained from the plants. The water was collected in tubs below so that it could be used again and again.

With all of these unusual changes to be made, the carpenters and other skilled workmen remained at work on the ship until well into September.

Oh yes, I should point out that the ship was stocked with supplies of food enough to last us for eighteen months. We had a large amount of bread and pork. Other supplies included sauerkraut, soup, malt, barley, and wheat. We also took aboard a number of animals, such as hogs, sheep, and poultry. These were not pets, you surely realize. We needed them for fresh meat. Men at sea must eat, you know.

And so let me say, "Welcome to the *Bounty*!" Next we shall meet a few of the people with whom we shall be sailing.

CHAPTER 2

Officers and Men of the Bounty

L ike me you probably know a great number of people. And you may have discovered, as I have, that when you met them for the first time, you would never have been able to tell what effect they would have on your life.

You are surely aware of the truth in what I am saying. Think about your best friend. Did you really think when you met that person that he or she would become so important to you? Is it possible that your best friend started out as your worst enemy? Such things happen. On the other hand, perhaps someone who once seemed likely to be a good friend has

15

now become unfriendly or uninterested in you. That also happens.

How little did I realize when I assembled my officers and men to begin our voyage on the *Bounty* what those men would later mean to me. There were some whose respect and friendship I was certain I could count on, but oh, how mistaken I was! Among the others were men who seemed to be less desirable shipmates. However, I would later find in them a courage and a toughness beyond my expectations.

Their faces appear before me once again. In my mind's eye I can trace each sun-darkened feature. I hear their voices, speaking in the rich language of the sea. I see them moving to their assigned stations on the ship, ready once more to sail. Ah yes, I remember the officers and men of the *Bounty*....

Perhaps you are asking, "What experience does Captain Bligh have that he should be put in charge of this ship?" After all, it was to sail many miles across seas that would present all kinds of dangers. My answer is that I had already made a voyage to the South Seas with the famous Captain James Cook.

I hope you recognize the name of Captain Cook. He was a great explorer of the sea. Think of him in the same way that you think of Christopher Columbus, Ferdinand Magellan, Sir Francis Drake, and Henry Hudson. Captain Cook made three voyages to the South Seas. The first one began in 1768 and concluded in 1771. It was on his second voyage, made from 1772 until 1775, that I was under his command as sailing master.

His last voyage took place from 1776 to 1779. He left England and made his way around the Cape of Good Hope at the southern tip of Africa. In 1777 he reached New Zealand. Later in this voyage, in 1778, he discovered the Sandwich Islands. He named these in honor of the Earl of Sandwich, first lord of the British admiralty. That is a fancy title, you may say. To put it simply the Sandwich Islands were named after a high official in the British navy.

Captain Cook sailed farther north and made other exciting discoveries, and then he returned to the Sandwich Islands to spend the winter there. Sadly, he was killed by the islanders there in 1779 as a result of a quarrel between his men and those islanders.

It pleases me to say that I learned the art of navigation from the great Captain Cook. That word "navigation" is, by the way, one you should know, along with its verb form, "navigate." It refers to the ability to find your way from place to place. You could say that you have navigated a horse or a handcart full of vegetables.

Of course, when I speak of navigation, I am particularly speaking of finding one's way across the sea from mainland to island, along coastlines, across stormy seas, past dangerous rocks, and the like. Even before the *Bounty* I

was able to practice such navigation. For a time I commanded a number of merchant ships in the West Indies.

I commanded a company of forty-three men aboard the *Bounty*. I will not attempt here to describe all of them and their responsibilities on the ship. But as I mention these few, pay close attention. You will be seeing most of these names quite a few times as you read my story.

John Fryer was the master. This meant that he was in charge of the navigation of the ship. (There's that word again!) Because his responsibilities were so important, his name will show up often in the account to come.

Our boatswain was William Cole. I trust that you are aware that that word is pronounced as though it were "bosun." Mr. Cole was responsible for keeping the deck in good order.

If I tell you that Mr. William Peckover was the gunner, you will have a good idea of what

20

he did. In the event of an attack, he would not have fired the guns himself, but would have been in command of the crew doing the firing.

Because Fletcher Christian, the master's mate, played a role later on in this voyage, I shall speak more fully of him. His responsibility was to assist Mr. Fryer, the master. This was Mr. Christian's third voyage with me. He had shown to me a great deal of ability. My confidence in him was strong enough that I put him in charge of the third watch on the *Bounty*. A watch, if you do not know, is a seaman's period of duty.

Mr. Christian comes from a very fine family in the north part of England. In no way did I have reason to suspect that he would come to cause me much grief.

I will mention here one more person, midshipman Peter Haywood. His family is also an excellent one from the northern part of England. Like Mr. Christian, Mr. Haywood pos-

sessed much ability. I gave these two men special attention, encouraging them to make use of that ability. It was my hope that they could become a credit to their country. But Mr. Haywood also would prove to be a painful disappointment to me.

Before I leave this subject, let me explain that a midshipman is responsible for passing along orders amidships, or from the middle of a ship to that part of the crew far removed from the captain. Besides Haywood we had four other men who handled this responsibility. It is interesting to point out that one of them wore the name "Hayward." I mention this so that you will not confuse Peter Haywood with Thomas Hayward, should I refer again to either man.

I spoke earlier of having a botanist on board. Let me tell you that a botanist is one who has a special knowledge of plants. He is able to identify them and is skilled in handling them. Of course, you already have figured out why we would need such a person. The gathering of the breadfruit plants and their care during the passage to the West Indies would be a good job for a botanist.

We actually had two men for this purpose, but I shall speak mainly of one of them. David Nelson had been with Captain Cook on Mr. Cook's last voyage and had labored at collecting useful plants. His experience would be an aid to us this time.

Another man, William Brown, was Mr. Nelson's assistant. Adding these to the captain, officers, and men of the ship brought our total number to forty-six.

Before I begin to tell you of our voyage, I must say a little about what my responsibilities were as captain. I was in charge of the ship and its crew. The men in my command were like all other men. They were sometimes tempted to neglect their duty or to disobey direct orders. Among a ship's crew such as mine one will generally find people with undesirable habits. Some may misuse strong drink. Others may engage in theft. Still others may be guilty of losing their tempers and taking violent actions. The list could go on and on.

Next consider that their duty at sea would take these men far away from the people who enforce the laws in their homeland. All this made it necessary for me as captain to exercise firm control over my ship. At times that control would require harsh punishment for the offender. I say this to prepare you for what lies ahead. In the following account you will see more than once how I had to order one of my men to be beaten.

But life on board a ship was not all work and pain. Seamen know how to sing, how to laugh, how to relax while off duty. So you need not be afraid. There are some pleasant moments ahead also.

CHAPTER 3

The Voyage Begins

The earth is a vast and wonderful place. One of the benefits of a life on the sea is the opportunity it offers to see more of the wonders of the earth. I would be an extremely restless man if I had to spend my life on a farm or in a tiny village or even on the streets of a great city like London. Let me travel; let me explore; and then I shall be happy.

Perhaps you are like me, wanting to see far-away lands and people with different languages and customs. If not, that is all right too.

Some people must stay in one place and grow our food and build our bridges and streets and ships and bring up children for England's future. But if you want to explore, it is a worthy dream. Do not let anyone take it away from you. Keep on dreaming it, and the day will come when you can make it happen.

I remember the day when we set sail. I looked back over the stern and watched England grow smaller and at last vanish. Then I turned and gazed out past the bow and dreamed of the wonders we would soon behold.

I still tremble with excitement as I remember those first days of our voyage. They were days filled with happenings, both good and bad. . . .

His Majesty, King George the Third, commanded that the earlier voyages be made to the South Seas. They were to serve the purpose of advancing the cause of science and increasing human knowledge. We would have these aims in mind as we sailed. However, it could be said that our voyage was the first one made with the intention of gaining some practical benefit from the earlier discoveries made by men such as Captain Cook. That benefit, as I have already explained, was the transporting of the breadfruit plants to a place where they could be put to a worthy use.

It was on Sunday morning, December 23, 1787, that we left Spithead on England's southern coast and sailed down the English Channel. Our voyage began with a series of troublesome incidents. On that very first afternoon, we almost lost one of our seamen. He was at work on one of the sails above the deck when he slipped and fell. However, he was able to catch hold of a stay, or rope, and was saved from serious injury.

Life on a ship, as you can quickly see, holds many dangers. But life anywhere involves certain risks. If you swim in an ocean, you may drown. If you ride a horse, you may fall off and injure yourself. If you climb a mountain or a high hill, you may slip and tumble back down. So whether at sea or on land you must be careful. The seaman who fell surely learned to be more careful.

We were able to celebrate Christmas in a relaxed and cheerful manner. Then, the following day we found ourselves caught in a severe storm. The raging sea broke into the ship, damaged our boats, and broke loose several casks of beer that had been lashed to the deck and washed them overboard. Later we discovered that the sea had broken open the stern and filled with water the cabin where our bread was stored. As a result, quite a bit of our bread was spoiled.

This period of difficulty gave way to several days of reasonably good weather. Then, on January 5, we saw the island of Teneriffe about ten leagues distant. Teneriffe is the largest of the thirteen islands known as the Canary Islands. They lie in the Atlantic Ocean, only a short distance from the coast of northwest Africa.

It is almost certain that when I mention the Canary Islands, you will think of the tiny bird with the cheerful song. You may not know that the canary is named for the islands, and not the islands for the bird. The islands received their name from the Latin word *canis*, which means *dog*, because early visitors found large, fierce dogs there. Dark green and olive-colored, the wild birds are found in abundance on the islands.

We anchored the ship near the town of Santa Cruz. I sent Mr. Christian to speak with the governor and inform him of our needs. We had stopped here to purchase additional food items and to repair the damages done to the ship. The governor answered politely that he would help supply us with whatever resources the island contained.

However, when I attempted to bargain for fruits and vegetables and meat, I was quite disappointed. Indian corn, potatoes, pumpkins, and onions were very scarce and therefore quite expensive. Beef and poultry were also difficult to obtain. The only fruit I purchased were a few dried figs and some bad oranges. I also bought water and wine.

We needed fresh fruits and vegetables, because of the danger of a disease called "scurvy." This is a sickness that men at sea often get. A person who has it can easily bruise or bleed. He will lose his appetite and become restless. And he could even die! I have been told that the Portuguese explorer Vasco daGama once had one hundred of his one hundred sixty men die of the disease.

It has been said that the juice of a lime can be a great help in keeping seamen from getting scurvy. For me, however, the important thing is to stop in ports often enough to obtain fresh fruits and vegetables. These seem to do well in preventing the sickness.

I was told while on Teneriffe that the population of the island stands somewhere between eighty and one hundred thousand. They have great numbers of vineyards, so that they are able to export a large amount of wine and a somewhat smaller amount of brandy. The growing of corn is also an important business, but they still need to import some of that vegetable. Trade arrangements with the Americans bring in flour and grain in exchange for wine.

The citizens of Santa Cruz, I learned, are generally free of disease. However, they, like so many other peoples, have suffered much from the breaking out of smallpox. This horrible disease has been known to kill as many as thirty of every one hundred people it attacks. Even those who survive are often left with scars for life. Because of this, they are very careful in Santa Cruz not to let visitors come ashore without showing a bill of health.

This concern about smallpox and other deadly diseases caused problems for a ship from London that arrived at Teneriffe the day before we sailed. This ship had brought no bill of health. The governor of Santa Cruz asked me if any serious disease was raging in England at the time our ships sailed. When I told him there was not, he allowed the people from the other ship to come ashore.

We sailed from Teneriffe on Thursday, January 10. Every person on board was in good health and in equally good spirits. I announced to the men that I intended to sail on to Otaheite without making further stops. That made it necessary for me to order a smaller allowance of bread for every person. Each man would now receive two-thirds of his normal amount.

I gave the further order that our drinking water should be filtered through dripstones that I had bought at Teneriffe. A dripstone is a kind of rock that is light enough that water can run through it. At the same time, the rock takes out of the water those things that make it impure. In this way we could avoid illnesses that result from the use of impure water.

As we moved out into that vast body of water known as the Atlantic Ocean, I thought of how man's knowledge of this ocean had grown. People of ancient times believed that a large island called Atlantis had once existed out here. The story was that mighty Atlantis had sunk forever under the ocean waters in one day's time. Powerful earthquakes and floods had brought about its destruction.

There were other people who once held the idea that the earth was flat. If a ship attempted to sail west from Europe, they feared that it might fall off the earth! By my time, however, nearly all people realized that the earth is round. We who were on board the *Bounty* had no concern about falling off the earth.

During the next several days we made good progress. When rains came, we were successful in collecting water to add to our supply on board. On one occasion the rain fell heavily enough that we were able to catch seven hundred gallons. You realize, I am sure, that seawater must not be drunk. Because of the salt in seawater, drinking it does not satisfy thirst, but only increases it. And so, while a ship at sea has water all around it, it must obtain its supply of drinking water before it sails, and after that, replenish its supply from rainfall.

The wet weather also produced a bad effect. Dampness causes mildew to develop, and creates a stuffiness below the deck. To combat this, we opened up the ship as much as possible during dry periods. We built fires below to dry up the dampness, and we sprinkled vinegar on several occasions. The men brought up their clothing and bedding to air them out. All this was necessary to avoid sickness.

With calmer conditions on the sea the men had time to make use of fishing lines and tackle. At various times they caught a number of dolphins, and on one occasion they landed a shark. You may not consider a shark as a fish you would desire to eat, but men at sea are glad to have any fresh food they can get.

I warned you earlier that I would be describing certain situations in which a member of my crew would require punishment. The first such instance on this voyage occurred on March 10. John Fryer, the master, complained to me about the behavior of seaman Matthew Quintal. He had been stirring up ill feelings among other members of the ship's company. I issued the order that he be given two dozen lashes.

The punishment was given with a cat-o'-nine-tails. This whip is made up of nine cords with knots in them, and these are attached to a handle. The reason for the name is that the cat-o'-nine-tails leaves scars on the body that look like scratches a cat makes.

The plan for our voyage called for us to sail first to the South Atlantic. We were to proceed around Cape Horn at the southern tip of South America and then to the Society Islands. Otaheite was one of these islands. By March 20 we were near Tierra del Fuego and the Strait of Magellan, which indicated to us that we were nearing Cape Horn. Over two hundred fifty years before, in 1520, the famous Portuguese explorer Ferdinand Magellan had discovered this strait. This was during the very first voyage made around the world. A strait, if you are not aware, is a narrow passage-way of water. This one is narrow indeed, ranging from two to twenty miles in width. It is also three hundred fifty miles long.

But we were not attempting the strait at this time of year. However, we felt that our chances of sailing around Cape Horn were good. At least, that was true until the morning of April 2, when a storm stronger than any I had met before halted our progress. It continued through the next few days, pelting us frequently with hail and sleet. With so much bad weather I found it necessary to keep a fire going constantly night and day.

The men were able to occupy themselves during this time with catching birds. Yes, I said birds, not fish. There were albatrosses, large white birds with darker wings and tails. These are greedy birds and therefore easy to catch with a baited hook. The men used the method of fastening on the bait a foot or two away from the hook. Then, when the bird took the bait, a sudden jerk of the line would hook it in the feet or body. They were also able to catch two beautiful kinds of birds, the small, blue peteral and the pintada.

At first the men ate the birds shortly after catching them, but they were not very meaty and had a fishy taste. So we tried an experiment, one which proved to be quite a success. By keeping the birds cooped up and cramming them full of ground corn, we were able to fatten them up in a fairly short period of time. In that way the pintadas became as plump as ducks, and the albatrosses tasted like fine geese. This extra supply of meat came, by the way, at a good time. The hogs alone had survived among our livestock, since the rough weather had been too much for the sheep and poultry to endure.

During this time our first persons were placed on the sick list since the voyage began. One of the cooks lost his footing because of the ship's violent motion; he fell and broke one of his ribs. Another man for a similar reason fell and dislocated his shoulder. And the gunner, Mr. Peckover, was laid up with rheumatism, or sore joints.

I finally concluded that it would be hopeless to continue our efforts to sail around Cape Horn. Had we been one month earlier we would probably have made it. Now, as a result of the almost unending storms, we had been in this area for thirty days.

On the other hand, the possibility of making it quickly back across the South Atlantic to the Cape of Good Hope seemed good. Strong westerly winds that blew in the South Atlantic made this a good choice. When I announced this decision at 5:00 on the evening of April 22, it was greeted with joy by every person on board.

CHAPTER 4

To the Cape and Beyond

To me it is a marvel how people of different countries have taken their turns at adding to our store of knowledge regarding our world.

We English have done our part. Captain James Cook certainly made some valuable discoveries during his voyages. But the Spanish, the Portuguese, the French, and the Italians have all given the world great explorers. Other countries, more than I can mention here, have given us information about this world we all share.

I remember being especially impressed by the Dutch and the great advances their people had made in the areas in which we were sailing. The Cape of Good Hope, New Holland, Van Diemen's Land, and other places we noted carried the marks of Dutch exploration.

We human beings are too often inclined to mock people from nations other than our own. I suppose that I have been as guilty as anyone of doing this. I have laughed at the way some speak and sneered at the strange clothing and customs of others. Are you guilty of that kind of behavior? Do you see, as I have come to see, how foolish a practice that is?

It is good to think back to our voyages, when we met people of various lands and races. I remember them all, the good ones and the evil ones, the friendly ones and those who turned against us. But I especially remember the fine Dutch people that I met....

We hurried across the South Atlantic, leaving Cape Horn behind us. We passed not far from the Falkland Islands. I felt that we had a good enough supply of fresh water to last us until we reached the Cape of Good Hope, so that it would not be necessary for us to stop at these islands.

I have been referring to capes. Perhaps I need to explain this. A cape is a point of land that projects out from a continent or island into a body of water. If you look at a map, you can see why the two capes I just mentioned are called that. It may be difficult for you to keep Cape Horn and the Cape of Good Hope clear in your mind. Maybe it will help to make the "e" in "Hope" stand for "east." We sailed east from Cape Horn to reach the Cape of Good Hope.

By the ninth day of May we were approaching the area where Tristan da Cunha lay. This is a name that you should speak aloud, for it is a delight to say—it is pronounced "Triss'tan duh koon'yuh." This name applies both to a group of islands and to one specific island in the group. They are located about halfway between South America and southern Africa.

47

I had intentions of making a brief stop on Tristan da Cunha, but in spite of clear weather we were unable to catch sight of it. When a night of thick rainy weather arrived, and we had sailed eastward of where the island was supposed to be, I gave up the idea of stopping there. So we pressed on toward the Cape of Good Hope.

At two o'clock on the afternoon of May 22, we saw Table Mountain, which forms a backdrop for Cape Town. We could have stopped in Table Bay, but at this particular time of year this bay is not considered safe for ships. Therefore, we sailed on to False Bay on the other side of the Cape of Good Hope.

We remained there for thirty-eight days. One reason for this was that the ship was in serious need of being caulked. That is, there were leaks that needed to be repaired and closed. We had found it necessary to pump water from the ship every hour from the time we left Cape Horn. Repair work was also needed on our sails and rigging.

Once again we needed to restock our food supplies. The leakiness of the ship had caused a great deal of food to spoil, especially the bread. This had to be replaced. Also, since the stormy conditions near Cape Horn had caused the deaths of our sheep, I looked into replacing these. However, the sheep I found were so

small and so expensive that I purchased mutton instead for the ship's daily use. You probably know that "mutton" is the name for the meat from sheep.

Our business in Cape Town was finally completed. We sailed again on June 29. The Atlantic Ocean and the Indian Ocean meet at the Cape of Good Hope, so as we moved in an east-southeasterly direction, we entered more fully into the Indian Ocean. Our next destination was Van Diemen's Land, located south of the huge, largely unexplored mass of land known as New Holland.

In 1770, when Captain Cook was here, he claimed for England a large portion of eastern New Holland. He named it New South Wales. It is now being put to some use by the British. Several months before the *Bounty* sailed, other ships left England on their way to New Holland. Captain Arthur Phillip had eleven ships and a cargo of people. It had been decided by the government to send to New South

Wales some 750 people who had broken the law. Many of them, by the way, were women.

A Dutchman named Abel Janszoon Tasman discovered Van Diemen's Land in 1642, almost one hundred fifty years before our journey there. He gave it a name that honored Governor Van Diemen of the Dutch East Indies. I had been to the place before with Captain Cook in 1777.

We sighted the island St. Paul on the morning of July 28. We did not stop at this island, although I would later learn that there was good fresh water on it. I was also told that the island featured a hot spring, which boiled fish just as perfectly as on a fire.

Several days later the rock named the Mewstone appeared, and this was a sign that the southwest cape of Van Diemen's land was only about five leagues away. The Mewstone is a very high, very remarkable rock that offers any ship passing this way a valuable guide in navigating these waters.

We anchored in Adventure Bay on August 21, near Cape Frederick Henry and about two miles away from Penguin Island. At this place I put to use one of the smaller boats we had on board the *Bounty*. I took this boat to look for a good place to find wood and water. Finding such a place on the west end of the beach, I returned to the ship. Mr. Christian and Mr. Peckover took charge of a party assigned to cut wood and draw water for us. Another man received a less attractive duty— he was to spend his time washing everyone else's clothes.

Mr. Nelson took advantage of our stay here to walk around in search of unusual plants and animals. He found a very large tree, which he measured and discovered that it was more than thirty-three feet around its trunk. On another day he came across a male opossum that had died of causes he could not determine. It measured fourteen inches from the ears to the beginning of the tail, and the tail was another fourteen inches long.

Our stay here also enabled us to add some different items to our food supply. From on board the ship we caught some fine rock cod with our lines and hooks. On shore we used a seine, which is a kind of a fishing net, but didn't have much success. Some of the men gathered mussels from the rocks and ate them. They suffered from a sickly feeling afterward, but I believed that was caused by overeating. We were also fortunate to find some tasty spider crabs.

At the same time we also attempted to improve the area for the benefit of future travelers who came this way. On the east side of the bay we set aside a few spots for the planting of some fruit trees I had obtained at Cape Town. We planted three apple trees, nine grapevines, and six plaintain trees. In the earth we placed the seeds or stones of oranges, lemons, cherries, plums, peaches, and apricots. We also planted pumpkins and two kinds of Indian corn. In order to identify where all of these were planted, for the benefit of those who would come here later, we marked nearby trees. Close to the place where we obtained our water we made use of a flat, favorable area for planting onions, cabbage roots, and potatoes. It was our hope that the natives would not in some way destroy all these.

We finally made contact with the natives in early September. I was disappointed that they had not come to us, so one morning we took a boat toward Cape Frederick Henry in search of them. Since we had seen their fires at night, we had a good idea where they might be. A curious thing happened as we waited offshore, watching for them. We were surprised to see William Brown, Mr. Nelson's assistant, come out of the nearby woods. He had wandered this far in looking for plants, and he had already met with several of the natives.

A little while later we heard voices that sounded like the cackling of geese. Then twenty natives came out of the woods and the greater part of them came on down to some rocks, where they were as close to us as they could get. There was no way that we could land, so I tied up the presents I had intended for them in paper. I threw these to the shore. They seemed to pay little attention to them. Then, when we pretended to be leaving, they picked up the presents and began to examine them. However, when we moved again toward the shore, they instantly put their presents back down and pretended not to notice anything that we had given them.

These natives were a dull black color, and they were covered with scars on their shoulders and upper bodies. They were of medium height or perhaps a bit shorter. One of them

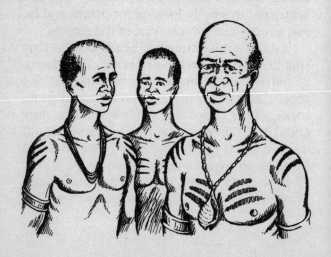

stood out from the others by the fact that his body was colored with red ocher—ocher being a mineral that can be ground into a fine powder for such purposes. The other men were painted a deeper black with a kind of soot. This had been applied so thickly to their faces and shoulders that it was difficult to say what they were like.

Because we could not land, I threw them a few more beads and nails, and this time they showed more interest. Some of them scrambled over rocks and reached out to catch the items as I threw them. As we left them, I hoped that they would come to our watering place. There we could become better acquainted with them. This, however, was not to be.

Later I was able to question William Brown. He was able to get a look at one of the men's homes, which was a rather poor wigwam in which there was nothing but a kangaroo skin spread on the ground and a basket made of rushes, or grasslike plants from the marshes.

CHAPTER 5

The Arrival
at Otaheite

I have found beauty everywhere. In England there are sights of beauty and wonder that I would not have wanted to miss. In London I think of St. Paul's Cathedral and Westminster Abbey. The puzzling ruins of Stonehenge and Dover's chalk-white cliffs, elsewhere in England also come to mind. And I experience a thrill when I merely picture the sun setting on an English meadow beside a tidy village.

There is beauty where you live. Do you have trees nearby? What marvelous objects they are! Do birds fly by your windows? Take a good look at their colors; listen to their songs; watch where they build their nests. Are there buildings where you live that have stood for many years? Give them some attention, and see the pride and care the builder put into his work.

I am convinced, however, that the highest form of beauty on earth is found in people. Have you discovered that? I am not referring merely to physical beauty, although that is of some importance. There is beauty in the way a person talks, the way he or she laughs, the way that person performs a duty, the way he or she responds to pain, and so many other ways. We need to look for the beauty in all the people we meet.

It was not difficult to see the beauty in the natives at Otaheite. Their childlike innocence, their generous gifts, the way they openly offered their affection touches me still. I remember the beautiful people of Otaheite....

My intention when we left Van Diemen's Land was to sail to the south of New Zealand, but the winds changed that plan. We sailed, therefore, toward the north of New Zealand. At daylight on September 19, we discovered a cluster of small rocky islands about four leagues distant from us. There were thirteen of them, according to our count. On them and near them we could see seals, penguins, many albatrosses, and a kind of white gull with a forked tail.

Captain Cook had been in this area in 1773, but he did not sight these islands. He considered New Zealand itself to be the nearest land. And so it was my privilege to name these islands. I called them the Bounty Isles, after our ship.

In this area we also saw a number of small fish called blubbers. These unusual creatures can be seen in the water at night because they actually give off light. They have something like strings extending from their body. These sometimes light up like the blaze of a candle, while the body itself remains entirely dark.

Thursday, October 9, was a sad day. We lost one of our seamen, a man named James Valentine. He had seemed one of the healthiest among our company until we arrived at Adventure Bay. There he began to complain of feeling ill. We believe that some sicknesses can be treated by drawing out a little blood. In James Valentine's case this did not help. The arm from which the blood was taken became painful and inflamed. Then the man suffered from a hollow cough and extreme difficulty in breathing, until at last he died.

Burial was, of course, at sea. It may seem a terrible thing merely to cast the body of a dead person into the ocean. But if you think about it, you know that it was the best thing for us to do.

At six o'clock on the evening of October 25 we sighted Otaheite. Knowing that we were likely to remain here for a lengthy time I ordered every person aboard to see the sur-

geon for an examination. It would have been tragic for us to have brought some terrible disease to the natives. The surgeon reported, however, that no such disease was harbored among us.

The following morning at daylight we entered Matavai Bay. A great number of canoes filled with excited natives were headed in our direction. They wanted to know if we were friends and whether or not we came from Britain. When we answered yes to both questions, they began to climb on board in vast numbers. We tried to prevent this, since we were still busy moving the ship into the bay. But in less than ten minutes the deck was so full that I was hardly able to find my own people. Finally we were able to anchor in the outer part of the bay and give full attention to our many visitors.

Before I relate any more about our welcome at Otaheite, I want to note that according to our log, we had run 27,086 miles from the time we left England to the day we anchored in Matavai Bay.

We now entered a world of remarkable beauty. The sky was pure blue, with the sun shining golden through it. On the nearby beach the surf made its continual lapping at the shore. Graceful palm trees stood beyond the beach. With their swaying in the breeze they seemed also to be waving a welcome to us. Even from here we could catch a glimpse of brilliant reds, gleaming yellows, and fiery oranges from Otaheite's many flowers.

But it was the people, the beautiful people, who were now closest to us. They smiled at us, greeted us happily, and looked over our ship with curious eyes. My knowledge of their language was not good, but I understood many words, and I was able to speak a little to them. What we could not say to one another, we could communicate with gestures.

Once the ship was anchored, the number of visitors continued to increase. Some of the

lesser chiefs came on board and gave us a few hogs. I gave them presents in return. The other natives brought a large supply of coconuts to us. But the product in which we were most interested, the breadfruit, was in scarce supply.

The natives asked several times about Captain Cook. They had learned from an earlier ship that had stopped here that he was dead, but they knew none of the details of his death. It did not seem like a wise idea to inform these natives that Captain Cook had been killed by other natives on the Sandwich Islands. Even before we reached Otaheite, I had ordered my officers and the ship's company not to discuss with the natives how the Captain had died.

One of the first persons I wanted to see or hear of was Omai. This man of Otaheite had gone to London with Captain Cook a few years earlier. His simple manner and the gentle way in which he spoke had made a deep impression on the British people. Some even went so far as to say that Omai and his people had a better society than the British. Without great cities or factories or fine homes or carriages or the like, they seemed to have a happier life in their natural state.

I was sad to learn that Omai had died. No details were given as to how he had died. The natives did agree, however, that it had been a natural death.

One of our visitors came on board with a picture of Captain Cook, which had been drawn in 1777. That picture had been left with Otoo, who had been the chief of Matavai when the Captain had last been here. The picture itself was in good condition, but the frame was broken. The natives brought it to me to be repaired. They told me that the Captain had suggested to them that whenever any English ship visited them, they should show them this picture. This, he had said, would serve as a token of friendship.

Early the next morning I received a message from Otoo. He was soon to arrive, and he asked that a boat be sent for him. I immediately assigned Mr. Christian to take a boat, pick up the chief, and bring him on board.

Otoo came to me with a great throng of attendants. He introduced his wife Iddeah to me, and then the chief and I joined noses. This is their normal way of greeting one another. In order to further seal our friendship he asked that we exchange names. In this way I learned that he was no longer called Otoo. That name had been passed along to his eldest son. He had now taken the name Tinah, and that is the name by which I will refer to him.

We exchanged gifts. I was presented a sizable piece of cloth, a large hog, and some breadfruit. In return I gave Tinah hatchets, small adzes, files, gimlets, saws, looking glasses, red feathers, and two shirts. To Iddeah I offered earrings, necklaces, and beads. However, she seemed more interested in what I

69

had given her husband. So I ended up giving her the same items.

Tinah and Iddeah wanted to see the entire ship, including the cabin where I slept. I was reluctant to permit this, but I went ahead with it. Just as I had feared, they were attracted to many things they saw, and I made gifts to them of several more items. As a result, they obtained as much more from me as I had already given.

When our walk about the ship was completed, Tinah asked me to fire some of the great guns. I gave the order for this to be done. The guns roared; the shot fell into the sea a great distance away; and the natives shouted in surprise and delight.

In the meantime, the people of the district of Matavai were bringing livestock in abundance for us to purchase. I appointed Mr. Peckover to handle this business, hoping to avoid any disputes. They brought hogs to us weighing two hundred pounds, and we pur-

chased several of them for salt pork. A number of goats were also for sale, so Mr. Peckover was kept quite busy.

It had taken almost no time for a bond of friendship and trust to form between us and the natives. The word used in Otaheite for *friend* is *tyo*, and in our first few days there, it could be said that every man in the ship had made a tyo. Tinah showed me a remarkable level of trust. When he left the ship, he asked me to keep safe for him all the presents I had given him. I pointed out a locker in my cabin that he could use and gave him a key for it.

Mr. Nelson had wasted little time in beginning the search for plants. At the close of this day he reported to me that he and Mr. Brown had already seen a number of promising breadfruit trees. It appeared that we were likely to be successful in accomplishing the main purpose for our coming to this island.

Before reaching Otaheite, I had instructed all the people on board the *Bounty* that they should not reveal to the natives our reasons for visiting Otaheite. I was fearful that such information might result in an increase in prices for the breadfruit. Perhaps I was being too cautious, but I wished to avoid any unnecessary difficulties.

I felt it would be a good idea to visit other districts on Otaheite besides Matavai. Therefore, I made plans for visiting Oparre, which is the district just west of Matavai. One of my reasons for going there was to see if Nelson would be able to obtain breadfruit plants there. In case we had problems getting what we needed in Matavai, it would be wise to be aware of other sources. I invited Tinah and Iddeah to accompany me on this trip, but of course I did not inform them of my true purpose in going.

During the trip Tinah expressed concern that I might be thinking of moving away from Matavai. He told me earnestly, "In my district you shall be supplied plentifully with every-

thing you want. All my people are your friends and friends of King George. But if you go to the other islands, you will have everything stolen from you."

I replied that King George had also shown him friendship by sending him valuable presents. Then I asked, "Tinah, are you willing to send King George something from you in return?"

"Yes," he said, "I am willing to send him anything I have." He began to list the items that it was possible for him to send, and in that list he mentioned the breadfruit. That was exactly what I had hoped to hear.

I told Tinah that King George would like the breadfruit trees. He immediately promised me that he would see that a great many breadfruit trees were put aboard our ship. It was clear that he was delighted to find it so easy to send something that would please King George.

This trip to Oparre featured one other notable experience. I had the opportunity to see Tinah's son, who had become supreme chief in his father's place. He appeared to be only about six years old, and he was attended by other children. I saw him only from a distance. He was on the opposite side of a river that I was not permitted to cross.

After returning to the ship I began to make more extensive preparations for the breadfruit plants. At daylight of the following day, I sent Mr. Christian as head of a work party to erect a tent on shore. I assembled Tinah and two other chiefs, along with Mr. Nelson and Mr. Brown, near the tent. With the chiefs' approval we set a boundary line. The natives were not to cross this without receiving permission. The chiefs would caution them against doing so.

This tent and others we would set up would hold the plants until we took them on board at the time of our departure from Otaheite. Earlier it would have seemed that we were asking the chiefs a favor by seeking to set up such a boundary line. But now it appeared that I was doing them a kindness by gathering breadfruit plants and taking them as a present to King George.

CHAPTER 6

Business on
Matavai Bay

The earth brings forth food in abundance! It fills me with wonder when I think of how God created this world and placed in it such a countless variety of foods for human needs.

Has it occurred to you how amazing it is that we can place a tiny seed of wheat in the earth, and it will finally give us many similar seeds that can be ground into flour? Another kind of seed grows until it becomes a tall apple tree, its limbs sagging with hundreds of apples. Still other seeds become round heads of cabbage, slender yellow carrots, and dark red beets.

A forest is full of food, and so is the ocean. The animals give us milk and eggs, and we use them for meat. Even tiny creatures like bees produce the sweet honey that we enjoy. You know all this, of course, but have you considered how marvelous it is?

And then, there is breadfruit. It is not the best food I have eaten. Many people would not like it at all. But for great numbers of human beings it is a very valuable crop and a much-loved part of their diet.

I came to know so much about breadfruit that some people have called me "Breadfruit Bligh." So how could I ever forget it and the labor that we put into gathering it?

Through the days that followed I showed Tinah the preparations I was making so that I could take the breadfruit plants on board. He was quite pleased with that, but he also reminded me regularly of other items he wanted from King George. Among the items he mentioned were large axes, files, saws, cloth of all kinds, hats, chairs, bedsteads, plus arms and ammunition. The list went on almost without end.

A serious situation arose when I learned that someone had stolen a part from the rudder of our large cutter—one of the boats from off the ship. I was disturbed by this theft and by other similar thefts the natives had committed. But I was even more troubled that these thefts resulted in part because of my own men's carelessness.

The thefts were bad in themselves, but even worse was the way they tended to interrupt the good terms we had worked out with the chiefs. I thought it would have a good effect if I punished, while they looked on, the man who had been assigned to guard the cutter. And so, with Tinah and several other chiefs present on the ship, I ordered that the man be given twelve lashes with the cat-o'-nine-tails. Before the punishment was completed, the chiefs were pleading with me to have it halted.

81

But this is a gloomy matter to discuss. Let me turn to an incident that is much more amusing and enjoyable to tell. The ship's barber had brought along a painted head from London. This is an object similar to those used in hair dressers' shops to show different styles for wearing one's hair. The head was made with the features and the coloring of a real person, so I asked the barber to dress it. He not only decorated the head, but he also draped some cloth around a long stick to give it a body. When this was done, we reported to the natives that we had an Englishwoman on board.

We moved the natives away from the part of the deck nearest the stern. Then we brought the "woman" up the ladder and carried her to that part of the deck. Some of the natives began shouting with excitement about this good British woman. A few of them, convinced that she was real, asked if she was my wife. One elderly native woman even ran up

them, the natives howled with laughter. Tinah and all the chiefs especially enjoyed the joke. It led them to ask me many questions about British women. They made me promise that when I returned, I would bring a ship full of them.

I should note, before leaving this incident, that the elderly woman who gave gifts to the British "woman" did not share in the delight over the joke. She was very embarrassed as she took back her presents.

Another amusing and interesting incident took place one day while I was at dinner. Tinah asked me if it would be all right for him to bring his priest down to my cabin for a visit. I replied that I would be glad to talk to the man.

My conversation with the priest naturally turned to religion. He told me they worshiped a great god called Oro, but they also had many lesser gods. "Did I worship a god?" he asked, "and if so, did he have a son, and who was his wife?" I answered that the God I worshiped had a Son, but no wife.

His next question was, who were my God's father and mother? I replied that He had neither father nor mother. The natives present all burst into laughter at this. They found it strange that my God could have no father or mother and have a child without a wife. I would have liked to explain my religion more fully to them and to have learned more about theirs. However, my lack of knowledge of their language made this impossible.

The warmth of the people's friendship toward me was shown again a few days later. I had been on shore at the tents, and I exposed myself too much to the sun. As a result I became ill and suffered from a great deal of pain for nearly an hour. The news of my illness spread quickly. Soon Tinah and many other men and women from among the natives gathered around me and offered their assistance. It proved to be a very brief illness, and I can say that I was almost glad afterward that I had experienced it. The affection and

kindness the people showed me at the time was deeply moving.

The weather had been unsettled for some time. One afternoon a storm began to blow into Matavai Bay. As the rain began to pour down and the waters of the bay began to churn, the ship rolled in a very violent way. Everybody remained on deck throughout the night, as we struggled to keep the ship from harm.

On shore another problem was created by the storm. The river that flowed into the bay began to swell and to flood its banks. Soon the point of land on which the tents stood was cut off by the waters and became an island. Because we feared for the safety of the breadfruit plants in the tents, some of the men cut a channel for the river on a part of the beach that was some distance away from the tents.

In the midst of all this activity I was surprised to see a canoe headed toward the ship through the rolling waters of the bay. It was Tinah, Iddeah, and one of the other chiefs. They handled the canoe with remarkable skill until they finally reached the ship. Once on board they embraced me and, with tears in their eyes, they told me of their fears for the safety of the ship and all of us on board.

Once the storm had passed, I went to shore to see how the plants had survived. I was relieved to see that they had suffered no injury. They had been carefully covered from the spray of the sea.

This was a sample of the rough weather we could encounter on Matavai Bay. From conversations with the natives, I learned that such weather was not rare in this place. I was therefore convinced that we should not remain in this bay much longer, so I began to make preparations for moving elsewhere as quickly as possible.

These preparations were interrupted by another occasion of sadness. This time it was the death of the ship's surgeon, who had been ill for quite some time.

I must say that the surgeon's illness and death were caused by his own personal habits. He was, first of all, a man who drank very hard. Like many before him and, I dare say, like many more to come, he destroyed his health by the careless usage of strong drink.

His other poor habit was what I can only call laziness. He hardly ever came out of his cabin. Because of that, we were hardly aware that he was sick. During our voyage from England to Otaheite, he rarely came up on deck. When he did, he took part in very little activity to exercise his body.

On the evening that his illness grew worse, we did perhaps the only thing we could do for him: We moved him to a place where he could have more fresh air. Nevertheless, he died about an hour later.

It was my desire to bury the surgeon on shore. Tinah helped me by gaining permission from his father for us to do that and by locating a spot for the grave. When I went with him to the gravesite, I took two men along to dig the grave. But I found that the natives were already doing it. Tinah had even made certain that the grave lay east and west, toward the sunrise and the sunset. He had apparently learned this practice from a Spanish ship that had visited Matavai many years before.

At four o'clock on the afternoon following the surgeon's death, we held the burial service. Many of the natives came to see the ceremony and paid close attention to what was said and done. They expressed some concern afterward about the danger of evil spirits coming around when a person died. I merely laughed and told them we had no fears regarding such spirits.

There remained one more detail to be completed following the burial service. I appointed Mr. Thomas Denman Ledward, formerly surgeon's mate, to do duty as surgeon.

My attention returned to the matter of moving the ship. I gave some thought to relocating in the harbor of Toahroah, which is east of Matavai. However, a period of fair weather over the next few days delayed the decision to move.

CHAPTER 7

The Move to Toahroah

Why do people steal? It is an act that brings a person into all kinds of trouble. Many thieves are caught and punished. Those who are not caught often live in fear of being caught. That would seem to make it unlikely that they would ever gain any pleasure from the stolen object.

And yet people still steal, and we all suffer in some way from it. It tends to damage the trust that has to exist among people living in the same society. It can cause us to spend too much time and strength in protecting our possessions rather than enjoying them.

Have you had something stolen that belonged to you? Then you know the truth of what I am saying. You did not trust other people in the same way afterward. And you were probably inclined to watch your property so closely that you missed some of the pleasure you once enjoyed.

When we entered the lands of people whose views of right and wrong were quite different from ours, we knew there was a good chance we would have certain items stolen. We did not regard it as acceptable behavior, but we understood why it happened. But when our own men were doing the stealing, that was a different matter.

It was a bitter experience when the deserters took some of our things from the ship and left our company. But I remember how we were able to discover where those men were and bring them back. . . .

Tinah and the rest of the natives were troubled by our plans to move the ship. They begged us to remain at least one month longer in Matavai Bay. Their obvious friendship and affection for us made me reluctant to leave them. But I needed to do what was safest for the ship and best for our task of gathering the breadfruit plants.

Before making my final decision, I sent Mr. Fryer in the launch to compare the depth of the water in the bay with that in the harbor at Toahroah. When he returned, he informed me that the harbor appeared to be the safer location.

We brought on board the plants that we had already collected. There were 774 pots, and all the plants were healthy. We had actually gathered over one thousand. However, when any plant showed signs of being useless to us, we rejected it. In this way we had thrown away 302 of them.

At daylight on December 25 we began our journey to Toahroah. It was with some difficulty that we departed Matavai Bay. As we

were about to get underway, we discovered that the ship's bow had run aground. We dropped anchors from the stern to help get us afloat. The cable holding one of the anchors was caught in a rock, and it took some effort to free it. But we were finally on our way.

When we landed at Toahroah the next morning, we were welcomed by a huge crowd. Tinah had come here from Matavai and had helped to prepare for our arrival. He showed me a house by the waterside. This, he said, was for our use. We were satisfied that it would serve us well here in storing the plants.

We had a problem with theft right away. Someone stole the cleaver used by Robert Lamb, our butcher. His own carelessness allowed it to happen. I complained to the chiefs on board about it, and they promised to make every effort to recover it. It was so valuable to the natives that I did not expect to see it again. To my surprise, however, Tinah found the thief and brought the cleaver back to us.

A more serious problem occurred on January 5. At four o'clock in the morning, when the watch changed, someone noticed that the small cutter was missing. I was informed immediately. When the ship's company was assembled, we found that three men were absent. One was Charles Churchill, the ship's corporal. The other two were seamen William Musprat and John Millward. They had taken arms and ammunition with them. We had no idea where they had gone.

When I reached the shore, the chiefs had information for me. The boat had been seen at Matavai. They told me the deserters had taken a canoe and were on their way to the island Tethuroa. I sent Mr. Fryer with one of the chiefs to search for the small cutter. They had gone only about halfway to Matavai when they met the boat. Five natives had found it and were bringing it back. We had to be thankful for the honesty and helpfulness of these people.

I told Tinah and the other chiefs that I needed their further help. The deserters had to be found and returned to us. We would not leave Otaheite without them. The chiefs agreed to help. One of them voiced some concern about whether or not the deserters had pistols. He felt that it might not be difficult to slip up on them and capture them, if they had only muskets. But if they had pistols, someone might be hurt. I assured them that the deserters had no pistols with them.

On January 22 I received a message that the deserters had been seen. They were at a place called Tettaha, about five miles from where we were. I took the cutter to the place. When I arrived at the house of the local chief, he told me the men were hiding in a nearby house.

With several of the natives joining me, I approached the house. I had my weapons ready, not certain what would happen. But there would be no gunfire or fighting. The men, having learned of my arrival, came out of the house unarmed and surrendered. I reclaimed the arms they had taken and left them for the night with the local chief.

Because of high winds and hard rains we spent the night on shore.

At daylight I sent for the arms I had left with the chief, and we returned to the ship. Mr. Churchill, Mr. Musprat, and Mr. Millward explained to me why they had so quickly surrendered.

It seems they realized their error in deserting. They had made plans for returning to the ship. However, they had to get past the natives, who were looking for an opportunity to seize them. When I came, they saw their chance to surrender to me. This also enabled them to avoid the disgrace of being brought in by the natives. One other problem, they admitted, made it an easy decision to give up

without a fight. Their ammunition had gotten wet and was therefore useless.

Two of the chiefs told me a somewhat different story. They said they had actually captured and bound the deserters. But the men had promised to return peaceably to the ship, so the natives had untied them. Then the deserters had escaped and regained their weapons. After that, the chiefs became more determined than ever to capture them again.

One problem was resolved, but another promptly came in its place.

I had to punish one of the seamen, Isaac Martin, with nineteen lashes. He had struck one of the natives. To me this ranked as an extremely serious offense. Even though some of the chiefs asked for the man to be pardoned, I saw that the punishment was carried out.

Still another problem was of a far different kind. A great number of cockroaches had appeared in the ship. Because of the plants we wanted to keep it as free of such pests as possible. And so one morning I ordered all chests to be taken on shore. Then I had the inside of the ship washed with boiling water.

One other kind of pest proved to be no problem. Rats and mice were killed off by the use of traps and some very good cats. Even on shore I hardly ever saw a rat. There had been numbers of them around when I visited here with Captain Cook. But a fine breed of cats left here by European ships had done away with most of them.

Our time at Otaheite was moving along, and after dinner one day I learned that Tinah had been thinking about our departure. He asked if he and Iddeah could go with us to England. It was his desire to see King George. He was certain that the king would also be glad to see him. Tinah was also very much interested in learning about other countries, and he wanted to see the other islands in these seas that we had described to him.

I could not allow the two of them to go to England with us. But I did promise that I would ask my king to arrange such a voyage later. Perhaps he would send me back to Otaheite in a larger ship. Then it would be much easier to fit in Tinah and Iddeah and the belongings they would take with them.

It soon came out that Tinah wanted to leave partly out of fear. He was afraid that as soon as our ship left, his enemies would attack him. Ah, Tinah, such a fine man in many ways! If only his courage were as great as his size and strength!

CHAPTER 8

Concern for a Cut Cable

T he sadness of parting—we all know what that is. You have probably faced a moment of separation when your mother or father, sister or brother waved good-bye and traveled out of sight.

We try to crowd as much as we can into those last moments together before the time of departure comes. A last kiss or embrace, a promise to write, a word of encouragement to be careful, perhaps a few tears—we are very familiar with these.

They are moments to treasure, for at such times we realize how much we love the person who is leaving. And we are more likely to express that love. Sometimes we may take him or her for granted; at other times we just assume he or she knows of our affection. But at the time of separation, we are much more inclined to say it: "I love you. I will miss you."

When we left Otaheite, it was truly a sad occasion. We had made many genuine friends among the people, and both they and we found it hard to say good-bye. But we could not stay any longer, because our work there was completed, and we needed to sail on to finish our mission.

I remember the day of our departure from Otaheite. I can still feel the pain of separation. The sadness in the eyes of the natives and their desperate efforts to keep us there just a little longer have left their mark on me. . . .

Our stay on Otaheite had gone fairly well, but on February 6 we faced a new difficulty. During the night someone cut the cable that connected the ship to the shore. Only one strand remained, and that was enough to prevent a terrible accident. But it was still a serious enough matter that I dealt with it as firmly as I could.

I had no question about Tinah's innocence in this matter. But when he came on board, I spoke to him in a very stern way about the need for his finding and bringing the offender to me. It seemed very likely to me that the act had been done by someone from outside Matavai and Oparre. However, I was angry enough that I frightened Tinah's parents. They moved from the harbor into the mountains.

Tinah and Iddeah remained with me. They were troubled that some of my anger was directed at them. Tinah promised to do his best to discover the offender. But, as he pointed out, if it was a stranger, someone not from Matavai or Oparre, it might not be possible to deliver him to me.

The person who cut the cable was never found. But since that time I have concluded that we were looking in the wrong place. Some of my own people were probably responsible. By cutting the ship adrift and allowing it to be driven on shore, they could have accomplished their purpose of forcing us to remain at Otaheite.

At that time such a thought never entered my mind. I knew some of my men had become very much attached to this island and its people. But I could not conceive of how strong this attachment was. How could I realize that there were men here who were quite willing to give up any intention of returning to England?

On March 2 we had to deal with another case of theft. This time a water cask, a compass, and Mr. Peckover's bedding had been stolen from the post on shore. When I sent a message to complain to Tinah, he did not come near me. But while I was on shore, I saw him, another chief, and a number of other natives marching toward the east.

Some time later the whole party appeared again. I saw that they had the water cask and the compass. Tinah was gripping the thief by the arm. When he tugged the offender in front of me, he suggested that I kill him. He went on to explain that the bedding had not been found, but he would search for it.

I thanked Tinah and the others for their assistance. This seemed a good time for me to make an important point. "It is a terrible wrong to steal from us," I told them.

They had seen how I ordered a beating for one of my men when he mistreated a native. Now it was only right that I punish a native who had done a wrong toward us.

Tinah stopped me from saying more by embracing me. He left to go look for the missing bedding. By these gestures he was telling me to do whatever I thought was best. I sent the man on board, where he received a severe beating. I was glad to discover, by the way, that he was not from Matavai or Oparre.

112

We had begun to make preparations for sailing. Tinah had supplied us with a good amount of firewood. He did this by ordering trees to be brought down from the country. This time he asked for something specific in exchange. Because he expected to be attacked after our ship sailed away, he requested some guns and ammunition. I agreed to this, but only when he assured me that they would be used only for defense.

I promised to leave him a pair of pistols. He showed no interest in using them himself. Iddeah would have one of them, and one of the other chiefs would receive the second one. Women in this country do not often go to war, but Iddeah was no ordinary woman. She was very strong and courageous. She also knew how to load and fire a musket very effectively. I felt certain she could also handle a pistol in a capable manner.

It was widely known that we were sailing soon. Natives from other parts of the island were coming and going constantly. This led to many more thefts being committed. Fortunately, nothing of great value was taken.

As always, these problems occurred in part because my men were neglecting their duties. You may be weary of the way I often criticize those under me. Remember what I said earlier. A captain must sometimes be harsh when his men do not perform their duties with care.

Toward the end of March we began to load the breadfruit plants onto the ship. They were in excellent condition. On some the roots had poked through the bottom of the pots. These would have shot into the ground if we had not taken care to prevent it.

At this point let me put in a word of praise. Mr. Nelson, Mr. Brown, and those men who worked with them performed their jobs very well. Because this was our major task to complete, it is good to be able to say that it was done well.

When the plants were all on board, we counted 1,015 of them. They were in 774 pots, thirty-nine tubs, and twenty-four boxes. We also collected a number of other plants. These included some other fruits, an excellent kind of plaintain, and some delicious pods from a tree that resembles a chestnut.

We spent our final evening on Otaheite on April 3. Tinah and Iddeah and his parents dined with me and remained on board for the night.

The ship was crowded the whole day with the natives. They loaded us down with their final gifts: coconuts, plaintains, breadfruit, hogs, and goats. As we looked out on the beach that evening, all was silent. Usually there was dancing and laughter, but not on this night.

At daylight we loosed the cable to the shore. Then we weighed anchor. With our boats we towed the ship out of the harbor. Just a few natives remained on board. Others were near the ship in their canoes. They begged us to stay just one more night.

However, I had decided that it was time to say good-bye.

After dinner I brought out the gifts promised to Tinah and Iddeah. These were placed in one of the ship's boats. There were the two pistols, two muskets, and a good supply of ammunition. I told them it was necessary for them to leave the ship now. That way the boat could return to us before dark. They parted with one last display of affection and a

116

word of blessing in the name of their god.

Tinah wanted me to salute him with the great guns when he departed the ship. I did not agree to this because I did not want to harm the plants in any way. But we did something else as a means of showing our regard for him. With all hands on deck, we gave him three hearty cheers.

At sunset the boat returned, and we set sail. We had spent twenty-three weeks at Otaheite. The people had treated us with kindness and affection, but that gracious treatment would produce some tragic results. For I am convinced that it was the friendship of these natives that would lead some of the *Bounty's* company to make a grave decision.

CHAPTER 9

Wind and a Waterspout

Have you known one of those moments when you feared for your life? Maybe you were cornered by a dangerous animal. Perhaps you felt yourself being pulled underwater while swimming. You may have taken a bad fall down a hill or from a roof. It is an experience you are likely never to forget.

In my lifetime I have been close to death several times from illness, accidents, and human violence. But I remember the day of the waterspout as an especially frightening one. To see the fury of nature wrapped up in a wildly spinning missile of air and water

119

aimed straight at me left my heart pounding for some time afterward.

I lived through it, of course. Like most of those occasions when our lives seem in peril, the threat of destruction passes us by. It was a reminder to me that we must not let fear rule us. It is likely that we will encounter many "storms" during the course of our lifetime. How much better to face these with confidence and courage, and to quiet the inner voice of fear.

The waterspout defeated me for a moment on that day when it advanced like a charging army at my ship. But I remember that I faced it and refused to let it beat me, and I gained victory over fear. . . .

A few days into our voyage, we met with one of the sea's well-known dangers. We had steered toward the Friendly Islands, west of the Society Islands. The plan for our voyage called for us to sail on either to Prince's Island or to the island of Java. Prince's Island was to be reached by proceeding through Endeavor Strait. This separates New Holland from New Guinea. If sailing conditions made that way unwise to take, then we were to go to Java in the East Indies.

Whichever of these we took, we were to go on by way of the Cape of Good Hope. From there we would cross the Atlantic. Our voyage would at last bring us to the West Indies. There we could complete our mission by safely delivering our cargo of breadfruit plants.

On the evening of April 9, our plans almost suffered a violent change. At nine o'clock we observed a body of thick, black clouds gathered in the east. A little later we saw a waterspout moving rapidly toward our ship. This whirling column of air and water looked like a dark, giant snake coiling toward us. I was able to see that it was about two feet in diameter in its upper part and about eight inches at the lower part. We needed to steer away from it, if possible.

The officers and men of the *Bounty* went into action. We changed our course and took in all but one of our sails. That action was taken just in time. The waterspout passed within ten yards of our stern. We heard its rustling noise, but we did not feel any effect from its nearness. Soon after passing us it began to die out.

This was as close to a waterspout as I had ever been. It is impossible to say what damage it might have done to us if it had passed directly over us. I imagine it would at the worst have carried away our masts. It is unlikely that it would have caused the loss of the entire ship.

On April 23 we anchored near Annamooka. Several natives arrived at the ship in large sailing canoes. When they came on board, we showed them our breadfruit plants and gave them gifts. We needed to obtain wood and water here, so assuring the natives of our friendship was important.

The party that went ashore to get the wood and water had some trouble. They had been on shore less than an hour when one man had an axe stolen from him, and another had an adze taken. The local chief was able to get the axe returned, but the adze was not recovered.

The men at least avoided one problem. When Captain Cook was here in 1777, many of his woodcutters were blinded for a short time

when they attempted to cut a certain tree. I am not certain if it was sap from the tree that caused the blindness or something else. For my men's sake, I gave the simple order to avoid that particular kind of tree. Can you imagine a tree being able to protect itself in that way?

Our troubles continued the following day. When Mr. Nelson went on shore to get a few plants, he was met by a group of natives who had no strong chief among them. They treated him in a very unfriendly manner and took his spade from him.

After our pleasant relations with the people of Otaheite, these problems were difficult to face. Perhaps it was good for us to be reminded that many natives on the islands of the South Seas neither feared us nor trusted us.

The watering party also had the anchor stolen from their boat. The local chief who had helped us recover the axe earlier was able this time to get Mr. Nelson's spade back. However, neither he nor any of the other chiefs present could gain control over the increasing numbers of natives on the shore. So I ordered the watering party to board the ship, and I decided it was time to sail.

As we remained offshore, some of the chiefs came on board. When they did so, I gave the order to sail. Then I told them that unless our anchor was returned, they would be kept in the ship. They were fearful of my threat, so they immediately sent men in canoes to find the stolen item. But they told me it would be impossible to return the anchor before the next day.

It was clear that we were not likely to see the anchor again. I kept the chiefs on the ship until sunset. By that time they had become even more fearful and upset, and they were quite unhappy that I had not allowed them to leave. They began to beat themselves on the face, and some of them were crying bitterly.

I was sure that they had nothing to do with the theft, so I told them they were free to go.

I gave each of them a gift of a hatchet and some other small tools. In a moment their distress turned to joy. They forgot all about the anxious hours on board, and we parted as genuine friends.

Are you concerned that we sometimes took advantage of the natives? Be assured that we always sought to form ties of friendship and trust with the people we met. When we

received something from them, we were careful to give something in return.

You have seen that I did not permit my men to treat the natives harshly or unfairly. However, we could not merely overlook wrongs done to us. If we allowed the natives to get away with theft or with damage to our property, any bond of trust between us would soon fade away. So we had to act firmly in situations like the one I just described.

Speaking of trust, I had found that I had placed a high degree of trust in Tinah and some of the other chiefs on Otaheite. And they had not broken that trust. I was about to have a very different experience with the trust I had placed in certain men of my own race.

CHAPTER 10

Mutiny!

❦

"Thou knowest not what a day may bring." This statement by St. James in the Bible is one with which we can all agree. When we awaken in the morning, we do not know what is going to happen to us. If we make careful plans, those plans may soon be forgotten. If we enter the day with a bit of fear regarding what we must face, sometimes the fear simply fades away.

What kinds of plans do you make? Well, I suppose you plan the study of your schoolwork. You surely have duties in your home for which you must save time. And you probably make plans for activities with your friends. It is important to prepare ourselves to make choices when our plans do not work out. We must be ready to try something different if things happen to us in an unexpected way.

I think that in a way I was prepared for that day when my plans changed. It was difficult to face a problem I had never faced before. But when the moment came for me to lose my ship and to lose men with skills I had counted on, I was ready to take a different course.

Certainly I remember that day. It was a day of great confusion and bitter rejection. It was a day that called for courage and the wisdom to make important decisions while under stress. It was the day of the mutiny....

Mutiny—it is a terrible word. Imagine a captain at sea having his ship taken from him by men no longer willing to obey his orders. It is something that never should happen. Yet it does happen, and it happened to me.

As Tuesday, April 28, 1789 approached, our voyage had been successful in almost every way. It was true that we had lost two members of our company. Three of our men had deserted for a time. There had been thefts committed by some of the natives we had met. But we had on board the ship over one thousand breadfruit plants. In our time at Otaheite, we had gained knowledge of the natives and of their languages and customs. Our voyage and the records we had kept would aid future travelers to this part of the world.

I was unaware, however, of a plot that had formed among the men. The carrying out of this plot would make our previous labors of little benefit. I am still amazed that I had no suspicions of the mutiny that was about to take place. The plotters had been very careful to keep all their plans and preparations to themselves.

The man who would lead the mutiny was Fletcher Christian, master's mate. The account

I have given has shown several times the kind
of trust I placed in this young man. His decision to betray me was one of the most painful
aspects of the entire experience.

On the evening of April 27, Mr. Christian
was to have had supper with me. He excused
himself, complaining of not feeling well. I
remember feeling concerned for his health,
but I had no concern regarding his honor and
loyalty.

On that fateful Tuesday, I was still asleep
shortly before sunrise. Four men, led by Mr.
Christian, suddenly entered my cabin, seized
me, and tied my hands behind my back. They
threatened to kill me on the spot if I spoke or
made the least noise. Even so, I cried out as
loudly as I could, desperately hoping that
someone from among the officers or men
would come to my rescue.

Mr. Christian and his three helpers were
joined by three others who had waited at my
cabin door. They hauled me roughly up to the

133

deck. I stood there in my shirt, suffering terrible pain from the tightness of the cords that bound my hands. When I demanded that I be given an explanation for this rough treatment, my only answer was a sharp order to hold my tongue.

I soon learned how serious the situation was. Mr. Fryer, Mr. Peckover, Mr. Ledward, Mr. Elphinstone, and Mr. Nelson were being held prisoners below. As I watched, Mr. Cole, Mr. Purcell, and Mr. Samuel were allowed to come up on the deck. Mr. Cole, the boatswain, was ordered to lower the launch into the sea. He was warned that he would suffer if he did not do it immediately.

When Mr. Cole had lowered the launch, two midshipmen, Mr. Hayward and Mr. Hallet, along with Mr. Samuel, were ordered to board it. Once again I demanded to know why all this was being done. I turned to Mr. Christian and urged him and the others to stop this act of mutiny.

Mr. Christian had been holding a cutlass. Now he asked one of the others to bring him a bayonet. These weapons may not be familiar to you. The cutlass is a kind of short sword, and the bayonet is a knife that attaches to a musket. Believe me, either of them can look frightening when held by men who have become your enemies.

Yanking me around by the cord that bound my hands, Mr. Christian swore at me several times. With the point of the bayonet aimed at my heart, he told me he would kill me if I spoke again. His various helpers had pistols and muskets cocked to fire. They seemed ready to kill me if he did not.

Several other men were ordered into the launch. It was becoming clear that I was soon to join them. Then, apparently, the launch would be left behind by the ship.

The mutineers allowed Mr. Cole and some of the seamen to collect a little equipment for sailing. They took canvas, sails, ropes, and the like. They also loaded onto the launch a cask of water, holding twenty-eight gallons; one hundred fifty pounds of bread; and a small amount of rum and wine. But only two items of equipment for navigation went into the boat. One was a quadrant, and the other was a compass. The maps, sextants, timekeepers, and other such equipment remained in the ship.

I will not attempt here to explain how all these items are used to navigate a ship. Let it simply be said that what was placed in the boat would be of little help.

The moment arrived for me to leave the ship. At that point I discovered that some of the men remaining aboard were being kept there against their wishes. Isaac Martin had been guarding me. The look in his eyes and the tone in his voice told me that he was not fully in agreement with this mutiny. He attempted to get into the boat after me, but the threats of the others convinced him to return to the ship.

Other men called out to me after I was in the launch. They wished to assure me that they had no part in the plot. Even Mr. Christian himself showed some brief moments of regret over what he was doing. As I was being removed from the ship, I asked him about the kindness I had shown him. "How could you pay me back for my friendship with this evil act?" My question troubled him, and he answered that he was in misery over having to do this.

I was thankful for the courage of Mr. Samuel, the clerk. Before leaving the ship, he was able to pick up some of my records and a few of the ship's official papers. He tried to take more, but one of the mutineers swore at him and shouted, "You are well off to get what you have!"

We did receive a few final supplies in the launch. Some of the men aboard the ship threw us a few pieces of pork, several items of clothing, and four cutlasses. They laughed at us and mocked us as they did.

The *Bounty* moved away from us, leaving us alone in the vast ocean. Still on board the ship were twenty-five men. It must be admitted that among them were the most capable members of our company. With me in the boat were eighteen men. That made nineteen men jammed into a vessel that measured only twenty-three feet in length. And besides men we had our food and water and our equipment in there with us.

Where was the *Bounty* headed? While it was still in sight, it was steering to the west-northwest. But I suspected this was meant only to deceive us. I had good reason to believe that the mutineers were going back to Otaheite.

It was not difficult to understand why the men would desire to return to Otaheite. They had enjoyed our six months there, and they might easily have concluded that to spend the remainder of their lives on that island would be far better than life in England.

The women of Otaheite are beautiful, graceful, and friendly. During our stay the men spent a good deal of their time with them. That in itself might explain why they would go as far as mutiny in order to resume their friendships with these women.

The chiefs at Otaheite had formed a close attachment to our people. To lure the men into staying, they offered them rich possessions. What a powerful temptation this was! The men could imagine themselves remaining on one of the most beautiful islands known. They could picture themselves having no need to labor, but simply enjoying plenty and pleasure for the rest of their lives.

And yet, I had no suspicion of how much that temptation could affect them. I might have supposed that some of the men would decide to desert the ship. After all, three of

them had attempted that while on Otaheite. But mutiny? That was beyond anything that I might have imagined.

I have tried in telling my story to do so in a cheerful manner. But how can I look back on the day of the mutiny with any kind of cheerfulness? Yet as I see it, matters could have been much worse. Think with me for a moment about what else could have happened.

First, I could have been killed on board the ship. I have described the weapons the mutineers held as they prepared to put me and the others off the ship. Had a fight broken out, I might have died on deck, the victim of a well-aimed cutlass.

Another possibility is that I could have been placed in the launch by myself. Without the company of those other eighteen men and without their efforts, I could not have survived.

And then, suppose the mutineers had sent us all off in the boat, but without food or water? It would have been a cruel thing to do. However, if someone other than Mr. Christian had been in charge, it could have happened. I hardly need to say that without food or water, we would have had little hope of preserving our lives.

There are other such possibilities, but what I have said is enough. I simply want to point out that a person in distress can always find some cause for hope and thanksgiving. From the beginning of this terrible experience, I looked for these positive features. I would find some way to triumph, and I would encourage the men with me to share in that triumph.

CHAPTER 11

Attack at Tofoa

❦

I have a knife that I have kept since that frightening day. It is small, and its blade no longer gleams in the light as it once did. I seldom use it anymore, but I will keep it as long as I live. For you see, it once saved my life.

We often overlook small things, but they can be very important. A book is a small thing, and yet there are books that have changed the thinking of millions of people. A wedding ring is also a small thing, but it helps to unite a man and a woman in marriage for the rest of their lives. A coin is still another small thing, but it can tempt a man to theft and murder.

Think about some of the small things you have: a book, a coin, a pair of shoes, a purse, and so on. You should keep them handy, appreciate them for what they can do, and be ready to use them when their time comes. They can be the means of changing your life for the better.

I remember the day of the natives' attack. We were in danger of losing everything we had—even our lives. But just when the situation was looking grim, that small knife gave us a chance to escape....

As I have said, the mutineers allowed us only a quadrant and a compass for use in navigating the boat. Both of these instruments did give us some help in determining the direction we had to travel in order to reach land.

The island of Tofoa lay to the northeast, only about ten leagues from us. My plan was to sail there and obtain a good supply of breadfruit and fresh water. Then we would sail on to Tongataboo. There I had hopes that the king, named Poulaho, would help us equip our boat and provide us with further food and water. That would enable us to sail on to the East Indies.

At first we had no wind, so we began rowing toward Tofoa. Late in the afternoon a breeze sprang up, and we were able to sail. It was dark, however, when we reached Tofoa. The shoreline was steep and rocky, making it impossible to land. We spent the night using two oars to hold us close to the island, but safely distant from the dangerous shoreline.

When morning came, we rowed along the shore. At last we saw a cove, a place of shelter and calm, where we were able to land. Mr. Samuel and some of the others went ashore to look for food and water. When they returned some time later, they had only a few quarts of water they had found in holes. Afterward, while again rowing along the shore, we saw several

coconut trees atop some high cliffs. Although it was a difficult task, some of the men climbed the cliffs and gathered twenty coconuts. That made one apiece for our supper.

During the next two days we continued our search for food. All we found were a few plaintains, and we collected about nine more gallons of water. As we searched, we also watched for natives. I had limited knowledge of this island, and I did not know whether or not natives lived on it.

On Friday, May 1, we finally met with some natives. About thirty of them appeared, and we bought a small amount of food from them. A few buttons and beads served as our payment. I had made up my mind to avoid using the bread and water we had in the boat. Therefore, for dinner I divided up equally among the men what we obtained at this time. It amounted to only one ounce of pork, one-fourth of a breadfruit, and one-half pint of water per man.

The natives were curious about what had happened to my ship. I hesitated to tell them what had actually happened. If they had known that part of our ship's company had forced us off into the boat, that might seem to them a sign of weakness in us. And if they thought we were weak, they could present a danger to us.

On the other hand, they were intelligent enough that I could not tell them just anything. For example, I could have told them that the ship was nearby and would soon come to pick us up. They needed only to look out from the hills to the ocean to see that was not true. I finally decided to tell them the ship had sunk, and we were the only ones who had survived. The men and I agreed in this story, and the natives appeared to be satisfied by it.

The natives continued coming and going during the afternoon. We were able to obtain enough breadfruit, plaintains, and coconuts to supply us for another day. But we received only five additional pints of water.

When evening came, we were left alone in the cove. I expected the natives to return on the following day with a larger amount of supplies for us. Then we would have enough to meet our needs on the voyage to Tongataboo. I planned on sailing just as soon as we could get those supplies aboard.

We ate a quiet supper, which included one coconut and one-fourth of a breadfruit apiece. I was pleased to see that the men were regaining an attitude of cheerfulness. Their earlier fear and discouragement were vanishing. They were ready to do their best to get us all to a place of safety.

In the morning two chiefs and a young man named Nageete paid us a visit. I had met Nageete at Annamooka on an earlier voyage, and I felt he was someone whom we could trust. Our visit was pleasant, but as we talked, I saw something that worried me. The number of natives in the cove was increasing at an alarming rate. Several of them were looking our way and whispering to one another. I was sure that they were designing a plot against us.

Suddenly several of the plotters rushed toward the line connecting the boat to the shore. They tried to pull the boat to the shore, but I quickly picked up my cutlass and held it up in warning. In that tense moment I asked one of the chiefs to tell his people that they should not bother our boat. He did so, and for a while nothing else happened.

My concern began to mount again after my men returned from the mountains, where they had obtained about three gallons of water. The natives were clearly planning an attack. We needed to finish our business here as soon as possible and leave this place. With that in mind, I bought all the breadfruit I could get.

A few natives offered us spears for sale, and I gladly purchased them. Up to this time the four cutlasses had been our only weapons.

But even with cutlasses and spears we had little hope of winning a fight. The natives had far greater numbers and weapons than we.

While we prepared to load the boat, we saw more and more of them lining the beach. Many of them were holding stones in their hands, knocking them together. I knew that this was the sign of an approaching attack. We

needed to leave quickly, but I told my men that it was necessary for us to wait until dark. If we had to fight our way out of this cove, the darkness would be a help to us.

We ate our dinner on foot. I was afraid that if we sat down, the natives would rush us and seize us. After dinner we began to load our things into the boat. The natives continued to gather in ever greater numbers. An attack was surely coming soon.

The afternoon moved by with painful slowness. The sound of the hammering stones never halted. Our ears ached from it, and our brains throbbed with each blow.

At last it was sunset. I ordered the men to pick up the remaining items we had on the beach and to board the boat. When the chiefs asked us what we were doing, I answered that we were going to sleep in the boat. In the morning, I added, we would come ashore again and continue our trading. One of the chiefs stood up and said, "You will not sleep on shore? Then we will kill you!" With that, he walked away.

The sound of the natives knocking their stones together was louder and even more threatening. I took Nageete by the hand, and we walked down to the beach. It was my hope that this man would help us to leave this place peaceably.

I watched the last of my men board the boat. Then I turned to Nageete to say good-bye. He urged me to stay here and speak again to the chiefs. But now I realized that he was not to be trusted. It was clear that he was working with the plotters. If the attack had begun at that moment, I would have killed him for his attempt to deceive me and trap me.

Nageete read in my eyes what I was think-ing. He let go of my hand and walked away. I boarded the boat, but as I did so, one of the men jumped out. John Norton ran up the beach and began to loosen the rope that con-

nected the stern to the shore. Mr. Fryer and the others shouted at him to get back in the boat, but it was too late.

I was no sooner seated in the boat than the attack began. John Norton was knocked down and struck again and again by stones thrown by the natives. Two of his attackers dropped to their knees where he lay and began beating him on the head with stones they held in their hands. There was nothing we could do for the poor man.

With stones flying at us from nearly every direction, we were all being struck and injured. In spite of that we struggled to make our escape. Several of the natives took hold of the stern rope and tried again to pull the boat to shore. They would have succeeded in this effort, but I drew my knife from my pocket and cut the rope.

The attackers were not about to give up. Twelve of them filled their canoes with stones, and took off from shore after us.

Pulling hard on our oars we moved out to sea. However, our boat was large and heavy, while their canoes were light and easy to handle. They paddled around us and renewed their attack. We picked up some of the stones that fell into the boat and hurled them back. But this had little effect. Our attackers were much better at this kind of fighting.

How long this might have continued, and what its outcome might have been, I am not able to say. At that point an idea occurred to me that probably was the key to saving our lives. I threw several items of clothing overboard. As I expected, the natives stopped to pick these up. When they did, we moved away from them. Because darkness was coming on fast, they gave up the attack and returned to shore.

We were once again at sea, nursing our wounds and struggling with discouragement over this latest misfortune. We had left behind one of our company, John Norton, killed in the natives' savage attack. He was a fine man and an excellent seaman, serving on his second voyage with me. I was very much saddened by his death.

Surviving the Sea

When will we human beings learn that we must work together to make a better world? We fight with one another, using words and often real weapons. We insist we are better than one another, and we let pride separate us from our fellow man. We mock one another and try to embarrass one another, ignoring the Golden Rule. How can we ever expect to find lasting peace and happiness?

I have seen an example of what it means to work together. When a boat at sea fills up with seawater, everyone aboard must bail. They are no longer captain and officers and ordinary seamen—they are simply a group of people trying to survive. Each one must do his part to bail out the water that can sink the boat.

It takes no remarkable abilities to bail out a boat. It is not what anyone would call a noble kind of labor. But it is something everyone can do and must do. That makes it like so many of life's tasks. People who lack outstanding skills and extensive training can still work together. By uniting their efforts at doing the simple jobs, they can accomplish a tremendous amount of good.

In my mind's eye I see again a boat filling up with water. And I see men struggling in the deepening pools forming in the boat. They were men of differing abilities, men who disagreed about many issues. But when their lives depended on it, they worked side-by-side to bail out the water. . . .

Our experience on Tofoa made it plain that my earlier plan was not wise. If the natives on that island were inclined to attack us, how could we be sure that those on Tongataboo would be any different? It occurred to me that the natives' friendliness toward us in times past probably resulted from their fear of our firearms. What would happen if any of these people were to discover that we had no muskets or pistols with us? They might not hesitate to take our boat and all our possessions from us. They might even kill us.

The men urged me to develop a new plan for getting us home. I told them our only hope now was to reach the Dutch settlement on the island of Timor. "That is," I admitted, "around twelve hundred leagues away. But I know of no other safe way that we can begin our return to our homeland."

Our new plan meant that we would sail near New Holland. Perhaps it would be possible for us to add to our small amount of supplies there. In case we could find nothing there, however, we would need to use very

carefully the food and water we had with us in the boat. And so the men agreed that each of us would live on one ounce of bread and one-fourth of a pint of water per day.

As we sailed away from Tofoa, we tried to put the bad experience there behind us. We thanked God for His protection and care, and we spoke to Him of our confidence that He would continue to help us. Making preparation for our lengthy voyage I divided the men into watches. This was a vessel at sea, and I was its captain. I felt that our boat should be put in better order. The men worked at arranging what we had, so that we could be prepared for whatever might happen.

The following morning quickly tested our preparations. We found ourselves caught in a violent storm. The boat was rising and falling in the wildly rolling waves, and the sea was curling over the stern. As the water filled the boat, we were in danger of sinking beneath the raging sea. Every man went into action, bailing with all his might. We used any container we could find to dip the water from around us and cast it back into the sea.

Saving our lives from the peril of the storm was one problem. But there was another, every bit as serious. Our bread was stored in bags, and it was in danger of being spoiled by the seawater. Even as we bailed, we had to find an answer to this second problem.

Mr. Purcell, the carpenter, pointed to the large chest he had taken off the ship. We opened it and took the tools out of it. There was now plenty of room in it for storing the bread. That was one problem solved.

I also had an idea to help us solve the more immediate problem of surviving the storm. We needed to lighten the boat. Therefore, I commanded that all extra clothing, other than two suits for each man, should be thrown overboard. In addition we threw out some rope and spare sails. This benefited us not only in lightening the boat, but also in giving us more room for bailing.

The storm continued throughout that day and well into the next. Nevertheless, I was soon confident that the boat was no longer in danger of filling and sinking. But the men were weary from the constant bailing. They were wet and cold, and their arms became so numb that they could hardly use them. I served to each one a teaspoonful of rum, which proved to be an effective treatment for these ailments.

During the next few days we encountered more pleasant weather. We found, however, that in spite of being placed in Mr. Purcell's chest, much of our bread had been damaged and was rotten. We ate it anyway without complaint, thankful that it had at least survived in this condition. One day we added a little coconut meat to the spoiled bread, and we drank the coconut milk. The allowance was only about two ounces of the meat and one-fourth pint of the milk. But this was a welcome change in our diet.

Food and water are two items we human beings often take for granted. The men on board the launch would not do that. In other times we also take for granted being able to walk and exercise our legs and being able to lie down and rest. These were pleasures that the men in the boat could not enjoy.

Our arrangements for sleeping were especially bad. I had divided the men into two nearly equal watches. That meant that one-half of them were sitting up, while the other half were lying either on the bottom of the boat or on top of a chest. There was no room to stretch out, so we were never entirely comfortable. The chilly night air and the unending wetness added to our misery.

As we were passing a cluster of islands, we were caught in a late afternoon downpour of rain. We all put our best efforts into catching some of the water. As a result, we were able to increase our overall supply to thirty-four gallons. And for the first time since the mutiny, each man was able to satisfy his thirst completely.

Once the rain had gone, we faced another time of severe suffering. Our clothing and our bodies were now wetter than they had been before. The cold air cut into us, causing a shivering that we had no way to stop.

When the sun came up again, we greeted a day that was fair and comfortable. Taking advantage of the sunshine and the warmth, we stripped off our clothes and dried them. It seemed a time to celebrate, so I increased our food allowance for this day. Each man received one and one-half ounces of pork, a teaspoonful of rum, one-half pint of coconut milk, and one ounce of bread.

That afternoon we cleaned out the boat. It took us until sunset to get everything dry and in order. In doing this we made a useful discovery. Several pistol balls had been accidentally put in the boat. I knew that twenty-five of them weighed one pound. Using two coconut shells I made a pair of scales. Then I announced that each man would now receive an amount of bread equal to one pistol ball. That meant that when bread was served, the allowance would be one-twenty-fifth of a pound per man.

It was during this time that I realized I needed to prepare the men for the possibility that something might happen to me. They would have had tremendous difficulty in navigating these waters without the knowledge I had gained. So I shared with them everything I had learned about New Guinea and New Holland and the sea that lay between us and Timor.

More stormy weather plagued us during the next several days. With no dry weather or sunshine, our clothing again became hopelessly wet. I recommended that each man strip off his clothing, soak it in salt water, wring it out, and put it on again. That probably sounds like a strange practice. I had learned in times past that it is helpful. It produces a surprising warmth, which one does not experience when merely wet with rainwater.

It occurred to me that the general run of cloudy and wet weather was not entirely bad.

Indeed, for at least two reasons, it could be viewed as an example of God's care for us. First, if we had experienced a lengthy period of hot, sunny days, we would all very likely have died of thirst. Being covered constantly with rain or seawater protected us from that awful fate. Second, the necessity of bailing out the boat may have been a cause of weariness, but it also gave us much-needed exercise.

I remember especially well Wednesday, May 20. That was a little more than three weeks after the mutiny and about two and one-half weeks after our hurried departure from Tofoa. At dawn on that day I took a good look at my men. Several of them seemed half-dead. The extreme hunger, the wetness and the cold, and the lack of rest was wearing every one of us down.

It was interesting that none of us was having a problem with thirst. Perhaps that was in part because we were developing a general hatred of water. We were usually covered with it. We had to lie in it while we were trying to sleep. And we had to spend hours bailing it out of the boat during storms.

There was another explanation for our lack of thirst. I do not remember whether one of the men suggested it, or if I thought of it myself. This explanation was that perhaps we were getting enough water directly through our skin, so that we did not need to take it through our mouth and throat.

May 20 was also a day when we enjoyed a brief period of sunshine.

It cheered us up for a little while. Then very early the following morning, the rain fell more heavily than ever. Once again our survival depended on our bailing with all the strength we had.

The rain stopped falling about noon, and the sun came out again. This time the sunshine did not make us feel much better. The sea was rough. Waves were breaking over the boat and keeping us at our bailing. This was an extremely dangerous time. We were forced to run the boat in the direction the sea was taking us. Even a slight error in steering would have resulted in our destruction.

After another dark, miserable night, I feared what I saw at dawn. Several of the men were so weary and weak that it seemed unlikely that they could survive one more evening like this. As this day continued, however, we began to see a change for the better. By evening the wind calmed somewhat, and we were able to relax a little. It was not a comfortable night, but it was improved, and we were thankful just for that.

On the following morning the sun came out and stayed out. For the first time in fifteen days we were able to enjoy its warmth. The calming of the sea and the fact that we did not have to bail gave us the opportunity to see how well our food was holding out.

I gave some thought to what we needed to do with our bread supply. According to the rate by which I had been serving it, I found that we still had enough for twenty-nine days. That was possibly enough to enable us to reach Timor, but I could not be sure. And then, we might not be able to stop at Timor but be forced to sail on to Java. That would mean six weeks, rather than four, remaining in our voyage.

I proposed to the men that we cut our allowance down further. It would mean less per day, but it would assure us of having at least a little bit if we had to go on to Java. As I spoke, I feared that some of the men would be unhappy with this idea. However, to my relief, they saw the importance of what I was proposing and cheerfully accepted it.

There was reason for hoping that we could obtain more food as we approached land. The birds that lived near islands might come close enough to us that we could catch them. They would not have much meat on them, but we were so hungry that we would not mind. We would eat the entire bird, including its head, feet, and all its inner parts.

You can imagine our excitement when we began to see some noddies. These birds were a sign that we were close to land, but we were more interested in the birds themselves. One day a few noddies did fly close to the boat, and we caught one of them by hand. It was about the size of a pigeon.

I divided it into eighteen portions. With that many hungry men waiting for a portion, it may seem that there would surely be arguments as to who was to receive the largest or the best. I avoided that by using a well-known method among men of the sea called, "Who shall have this?"

With this method, one person turns his back on the food to be divided. Another individual then points to one of the portions and asks, "Who shall have this?" The person with his back turned then names one member of the group waiting to receive portions. In this manner each portion is finally passed out, and everyone has had an equal chance at getting the best share.

Later that day and again the next day we were able to catch three more birds. These were all of a kind known as "boobies." Two of them provided more food than we expected. When we cut their stomachs open, we found several flying fish and small cuttlefish in them.

Flying fish, by the way, do not actually fly. When they leap out of the water, they are able to hold their fins in such a way that they glide through the air. The cuttlefish is not really a fish but an animal related to the octopus. Like the octopus it can release a substance like ink from its body to escape an enemy.

Both the flying fish and the cuttlefish may be eaten. However, most people prefer eating their seafood before it has been eaten by some other animal or bird.

While I am at it, let me also tell you a little more about noddies and boobies. They both received their names from seamen.

They are foolish creatures that allow themselves to be caught easily on the rigging of ships. The booby is as large as a duck and provides nearly as much meat.

By the time we had divided the two, plus the fish from their stomachs, into eighteen parts and had added the daily portions of bread and water, we had a feast. At least, all the men regarded it as a feast.

As we neared New Holland, we faced a new problem. This was one that I felt confident we could handle. The eastern coast of New Holland is fenced off by a lengthy barrier of reefs. These are ridges of rock formed, I am told, by the bodies of millions of tiny animals. They can, of course, be quite dangerous if a boat should strike them as a reef can tear a

large hole in the bottom of the boat. However, I believed that we could find an opening in them, and then we could pass through into smoother waters.

In spite of some difficulty, we did locate a break in the reef. We all felt a fresh sense of joy as we entered smooth waters, smooth because the reef shelters them from the ocean. I announced to the men we would land on the first safe-looking piece of shoreline we saw. At this point all of the hardships we had recently suffered seemed already to be forgotten.

Once again we offered our prayers of thanksgiving to God for the gracious protection we had received. It was with a deep sense of contentment that we shared our dinner, although it was only one-twenty-fifth of a pound of bread and one-fourth of a pint of water.

CHAPTER 13

From Island to Island

Alone, with no sound of church bells ringing or carriage wheels rattling by or children's voices echoing in the streets… alone, with only surf and sunshine, breezes and birds to interrupt the continual silence… alone, with only the seventeen familiar faces of your companions at which to gaze. This I remember from the few days we spent among the islands off New Holland.

You can discover a number of benefits in being alone for a while. It gives you time for serious thinking. There are no people or noise to distract you. You can think about who you really are and why God has placed you on this earth. You can call to mind all those people who are dear to you and consider how you can show them your love. You can set goals for the future and work out careful plans for reaching those goals.

One of the richest benefits in being alone is that it helps us to appreciate the fact that we are not alone all the time. I have enjoyed moments of being alone, but I am glad that afterward I was able to be with family, friends, and other men of the sea.

I remember the lonely islands of New Holland. In those few days that we spent there we had plenty of time to think and to plan. I am thankful now for those days, but I am also thankful that they are a part of my past. . . .

Our first stop was at an island on which we found a bay and a fine sandy point. The first thing we did upon landing was to look for signs of natives. Finding no evidence to indicate they were nearby, we spent the night in this place and enjoyed a calm and peaceful rest.

We greeted the new day with a hope that would not have seemed possible a few days earlier. While search parties were out looking for food and water, those of us who stayed by the boat made a striking discovery. It reminded us afresh how much we were under God's care. During the previous night an important part from the boat's rudder had come out and was lost.

On a ship or boat, the rudder is the device by which the vessel is steered. It can easily be seen, then, that a damaged rudder is a serious problem indeed. In our case the lost piece would have made the rudder practically useless. We were thankful that this accident had not happened while we were still at sea. With the rolling, tossing seas that we had battled, a useless rudder would have caused our destruction. But now we were able to make use of a large staple in the boat to repair the damage.

There was further evidence of God's care when the search parties returned. They had found a large number of oysters and plenty of fresh water. By using a magnifying glass I made a fire. We had a copper pot in the boat, which one of the men had been wise enough to bring from the ship. With this we were able to prepare a stew, using the oysters, some bread, and a little pork. Each person received a full pint of this tasty mixture.

While I had the fire going, I used two more items found in the boat. One was a tinderbox, and the other a piece of brimstone. We could use these to make sure we would have fire for future use.

If you are not familiar with a tinderbox, I will be glad to explain. This box holds a piece of tinder, which is a material that will easily catch fire. It may be linen or cotton or the bark from certain trees. Whatever the material, it must be heated in an oven until it is almost ready to burn. Then it is placed in a

tinderbox, where it is kept dry. The box also contains pieces of flint and steel, which when struck together will produce a spark. The spark lights the tinder and when other kindling or burnable material is added, one can build a good fire.

Getting water for our needs here proved to be an easy matter. We were actually able to dig a well. At a certain spot we noticed some wire grass, which indicated that water was beneath the ground. When we pushed a stick about three feet long into the ground, we found a good supply of water. The well we dug did not need to be very deep, but it provided all the water we wanted.

This island also provided a rich variety of foods. Besides the oysters we ate the soft inner heart that we cut out of the tops of some palm trees. Mr. Nelson found some fern roots that were juicy enough to help satisfy thirst. They were useful to any person who wanted something other than water. I thought at first these might be roasted and serve as a substitute for bread, but that idea did not work out.

There were also three kinds of berries we were able to eat. Berries can be poisonous, so I warned the men to avoid eating any that they found. But when they began to roam the island, they forgot my warning and ate heavily of the three kinds. A few of them ate so many berries that they became sick. This caused some fear that these berries were poisonous. But the sickness passed, and then we saw that birds were eating the same fruit. That gave us confidence that we could safely eat them also.

One kind was similar in size to a large gooseberry, with a sweet taste. It grew on a small vine and had a pale red skin streaked with yellow. Another grew on bushes, and the fruit formed in clusters like elderberries. The third was a blackberry, but we did not find as many of this kind as we did the others.

The morning of Saturday, May 30, was our third day on what I had decided to call "Restoration Island." It seemed a fitting name because the good food and fresh water here were restoring our health and strength. And, of course, we were also able to rest here in a way that had been impossible while we were at sea.

However, we had a voyage to complete, so I made plans to put out to sea again. The men went out to gather as many oysters as they

could. While they were gone, I filled all the boat's water vessels. That gave us nearly sixty gallons with which to begin the next portion of our journey.

For our dinner I served the last of our pork. My intention in this was partly to prevent any further stealing from the supply. Someone from our company had been taking it while I was away from the boat. We had our normal allowance of bread with the pork.

In the afternoon we spent a period of time in prayer together. At four o'clock we were about ready to sail when some natives appeared on the shore across from us. There were perhaps twenty of them. They were naked and black, with short, bushy hair. Each was carrying a spear in his right hand and a shorter weapon in his left hand.

I suppose we all recalled at that moment what had happened at Tofoa. But these natives had no canoes with them. They gestured to us that they wanted us to land where they were, but we turned our eyes to the sea and left them behind us.

On the following day we landed on the rocky shore of a second island. I divided the men into three parties. One was to search to the north for food. I ordered the second one to head south and also look for food. The third group was to remain by the boat. These were simple orders, but when I gave them, the men stood their ground.

A few of the men began to grumble. They spoke harsh words to one another and to me. One of the men went so far as to challenge me. He declared that he was as good a man as I was.

I saw that I would have to act boldly if I were to remain in command. Seizing a cutlass I ordered the man to pick up one of the other cutlasses and prepare to defend himself. He was surprised by my action and unable to speak for a moment. When he did, he complained that I wanted to kill him. But he backed off from his challenge. In a few minutes everything was quiet again. The men then set out to perform the duties assigned them.

I named this island "Sunday Island," since we had arrived here on that day. It was not a place where we would stay for long. There was little protection for us if natives were to attack us in canoes. Furthermore, I saw another small island not far away that I felt would be a better place to spend the night, so we prepared to sail there.

When we reached this next island, it was just getting dark. We discovered that a reef lay between us and the shore. It would have been risky to work through this in the dark, so we put out our anchor and spent the night in the boat.

At dawn we made our way to shore and were encouraged when we saw turtle tracks. Also, we noted that a great number of noddies apparently nested on this island. Therefore, it seemed that we would be able to obtain an abundance of food here. When our search parties returned, though, they had only a few clams and some dolichos. This strange-sounding food is a kind of bean that Mr. Nelson located. Adding all these to some oysters we had collected at Sunday Island, we were able to have a fairly good dinner.

Some of the men became sick in the afternoon, and they were inclined to suspect the dolichos were the cause. Mr. Nelson was especially ill. His sufferings included severe physical weakness, an inability to walk, and loss of sight for a brief time. Part of his problem, I knew, was his failure to take a little rest in the shade. He was always pressing on with his work beyond what his strength allowed. He did not have a fever, and I was relieved to see him respond to my treatment. That was merely a few doses of wine with pieces of bread soaked in it.

Mr. Cole and Mr. Purcell complained of headaches and of being sick to their stomachs.

Others among the men were also suffering. I doubted that the dolichos were the cause because I and a few others had eaten them and suffered no ill effects. It was more likely that the sickness resulted from eating the dolichos raw. I believe that those who complained of sickness had done that.

In the evening I warned the men to make sure they kept their fires small. We did not want any natives in the area to know of our location. While I strolled up and down the beach to see if anyone on the nearby mainland was likely to know we were here, I left Mr. Samuel and Mr. Peckover in charge of making certain my order regarding fires was heeded.

All of a sudden the sky lit up as though the entire island were ablaze. I rushed back to the men to see what had happened. I found that one of the men had chosen to be foolish and stubborn. He had moved away from the others and built his own personal fire. Continuing his foolish behavior, he built his fire too close to some dry grass and set it afire. The rapidly spreading flames had produced enough light to be seen for miles. Now we had to worry again about an attack by natives. If they did attack, we were not strong enough or well-armed enough to save ourselves.

Before we left this island, we made one further attempt to add to our food supply. Mr. Samuel and Mr. Peckover went out to look for turtle, but in spite of a thorough search they were not successful. Three other men were assigned to catch birds. They returned later with twelve noddies, which was not much. You may remember I mentioned earlier that a noddy is equal in size to a pigeon.

The number of birds these men caught could have been greater. One of the men, Robert Lamb, separated himself from the other two. As they closed in on the birds, Lamb made so much noise and unnecessary movement that quite a few of the noddies were frightened and flew away.

Lamb's careless behavior made me so angry that I gave him a sound beating. Much later I would learn that during the time he was separated from the other two men, he ate nine birds raw.

At sunset on June 2 we approached another island. This one I called "Turtle Island." However, the search party I sent ashore found only a large number of turtle bones and shells. These were apparently the remains of a recent feast by the natives. We slept in the boat overnight, and at daylight we resumed our voyage through the islands of New Holland.

Our last stop before launching into the open sea was a small rocky island that I named "Booby Island" because of seeing many of those birds there. I would later discover that Captain Cook had seen this island and had given it the same name.

CHAPTER 14

At Last—Timor!

P eople tell me I did an amazing thing. To sail so far in a small vessel, with only the simplest tools for navigation—they marvel at that. I have achieved a certain measure of fame for that, aside from my role in connection with the mutiny.

For me it was only a matter of setting a goal and reaching it. If we had decided that we would merely sail until we happened to find an island with friendly people, we would surely have perished. Instead, we made up our minds exactly where we wanted to go. Then we determined what we had to do to get there, and we did it.

I have found that this is the wise way of approaching any kind of task. Set your goal; figure out what you must do to reach it; and get to work. Once you fulfill one goal, then set another, and follow the same steps. In this way you can accomplish many worthwhile things.

And oh, the thrill of reaching a goal! You have a chance to feel the excitement I felt when the island of Timor came into view. I remember clearly that heart-pounding experience from days long past....

It was eight o'clock on the evening of June 3 when we left the islands of New Holland behind. I encouraged the men by expressing hope that in eight to ten days we would reach a land of safety. After praying to God that He would continue to grant us His protection, I served an allowance of water alone for supper.

As I looked back over the six days we had spent near the coast of New Holland, I had to admit that we had gathered only a small amount of food. But we had enjoyed one very important benefit: rest. For a little while we had been freed from the weariness of being constantly in the boat, and we had been able to sleep much more comfortably at night. The time we spent there improved our health and raised our hopes of survival. Without it many of the men might have given up the struggle. It is likely that we would have left behind several fresh graves on those islands.

Once again we encountered the problems of a sea running high and filling the boat with seawater. Once again we met with frequent showers of rain. We endured several days of wet bodies and wet clothing and nights of shivering in the cold.

The general improvement in health was quickly reversed. I grew concerned for the surgeon, Mr. Ledward, and for Lawrence Lebogue, a tough old seaman. Both appeared to be giving way very fast. The only means I had for treating them in their weakness was a teaspoonful or two of the wine, which I had saved for such a purpose.

Our supply of food, never large, began to get smaller and smaller. I was able to add something to it one evening when I caught a booby with my hands. I divided the bird's blood among three of the men who seemed to be the weakest. We used the "Who shall have this?" method once again for passing out the portions of its body. One afternoon we caught a small dolphin, which we used for two meals. My portion of this food made me sick, since the share I received came from its stomach.

Wednesday morning, June 10, was another of those occasions that I remember especially well. I looked over all of my men and was very worried about their appearance. They were suffering from extreme weakness. Their legs were swollen, and their faces were hollow from lack of rest. They seemed to be having quite a bit of difficulty in understanding my words.

Mr. Ledward and Lawrence Lebogue were still the ones in the poorest condition, and I continued to give them teaspoonfuls of the small amount of wine that remained. I say they were in the poorest condition, but not everyone shared that opinion. At one point Mr. Cole took a long look at me, and, in a tone of voice that was perfectly sincere, he told me that I looked worse than anyone else in the boat. Instead of being offended I actually laughed at that. I made sure to give Mr. Cole a similar compliment.

It was three o'clock in the morning on June 12 when we sighted Timor. Its shoreline was about two leagues from us. There is no way that I can describe the joy we all felt when we caught sight of this land. We had come, according to our log, 3,618 miles from Tofoa to Timor in forty-one days. During that voyage, in spite of many occasions of distress, we had not lost one man. Only John Norton, killed by the natives at Tofoa, was missing from the nineteen who had been ordered off the *Bounty* and into the launch.

Of course we had not yet reached a place of safety. I did not know where the Dutch settlement was located on this island. Even here we could not be certain that all the natives were friendly. Some of my men were in favor of landing immediately, but I told them it would not be wise.

It seemed to me that I had once been told that the Dutch settlement was on the southwest side of the island. So I gave the order to sail along shore to the south-southwest. As we moved along the shore, we gained a good deal of pleasure in seeing woods and lawns and what seemed to be fields and gardens. But, as far as human dwellings were concerned, we observed only a few small huts. The farther we sailed, the more I was inclined to believe that I had been mistaken about the settlement's being in this area.

During the afternoon we continued our course along the shore. I was already making the change from a man whose only thought was survival to a person who was eager to learn about the world he was seeing. For that reason I paid particular attention to a number of palm trees that we passed. I recognized them as fan palms. They are named for their leaves, which spread out like fans.

For a long time we saw no other signs of human activity. Finally we observed several columns of smoke. We agreed that these may have resulted from people's clearing land so that they could grow crops on it.

As evening came, I was concerned about the danger of running past the settlement during the darkness. We stopped our search and spent the night about half a league from shore. Our excitement at reaching Timor was as great as ever. But it was clear that we were going to have to add a good dose of patience to it.

We resumed our search in the morning. It was about two o'clock in the afternoon when we discovered a spacious bay, with an entrance about two or three miles wide. I thought that surely our voyage was now almost finished. After all, this bay appeared to be a perfect location for the Dutch settlement. Again, however, I would not be correct.

We anchored in a small, sandy bay near the east side of the entrance to the larger bay. Not far away we saw a hut with a dog and some cattle close to it. I immediately sent Mr. Cole and Mr. Peckover to the hut to see if they could obtain the information we needed.

A few minutes later the two men returned with five natives, who were members of two families. Their polite manner convinced us that they must have spent a good deal of time in contact with Europeans. They explained that the Dutch governor resided at a place called Coupang, which was located to the northeast a good distance from here. I used signs to indicate to one of the natives that I would be willing to pay him if he would show us the way to Coupang. He promptly agreed and boarded the boat.

These people were very kind to us. Before we departed, they brought us a few pieces of dried turtle meat and some ears of Indian corn. We were able to enjoy the corn, but not the turtle meat. It was so hard that it could not be eaten until it was soaked in hot water.

One interesting habit of these natives was their chewing of betelnut. This is the seed of a palm tree, which is boiled and dried and then rolled in a leaf of the betel vine. When it is chewed, it turns the chewer's mouth red and sometimes blackens his teeth. Each of the natives we saw had a handkerchief hanging by the four corners from his shoulders, which served as a bag to hold his betelnut.

With our pilot ready to show the way, we sailed at half past four. We worked our way along an eastern shore until ten o'clock, when we dropped our anchor. For the first time I issued a double allowance of bread and a little wine to each man. Then we enjoyed a very restful sleep until one o'clock in the morning, when we resumed our journey.

Not much later we heard two cannons fire. Now we were more alert and expectant than ever. Soon we saw three ships, two of them

square-rigged vessels and the other a cutter lying at anchor. Having difficulty with the wind we took to our oars and rowed for a while. Then we rested and ate and rowed again until we found ourselves approaching a small fort and town. The pilot told me this was Coupang.

It occurred to me that it would be improper for us to try to land without receiving permission. Therefore, I raised a signal of distress, and we tried to be patient in waiting. Shortly after daybreak a soldier gestured for us to land. When we did, we were surprised to meet, among a crowd of natives, an English sailor. He told us he belonged to one of the vessels we had seen. I also learned from him that his captain was next in authority here to the Dutch governor. He explained to me that the governor was ill and could not see me. When I heard that, I promptly requested to meet with the captain.

Captain Spikerman acted quickly after I informed him of our terrible situation. He gave orders that my men were to be taken to his own house. As they came ashore, some of them barely able to walk, the people of Timor watched us in horror. We looked more like ghosts than living human beings. Our bodies were nothing but skin and bones; our arms and legs were covered with sores; and we were clothed in rags. It was with tears of grat-

213

itude and joy in our eyes that we made our way into Captain Spikerman's house. There a breakfast of tea with bread and butter awaited us.

In spite of his illness the governor, Mr. William Adrian Van Este, agreed to see me as soon as possible. When I entered his house, he gave me a very kind welcome. With genuine sincerity he expressed his sorrow at all the trials through which my men and I had suffered. Then he made a statement I especially remember. He told me that he regarded it as the greatest blessing of his life that he had the means of giving us aid. Before I left, he promised me a house and assured me that lodging would also be provided for my men.

After I finished speaking with the governor, I asked to see the house he had promised me. I found it ready for my use, with servants assigned to assist me. The house contained a large hall, with a room at each end and a loft overhead. It was surrounded by a porch, with an outer apartment in one corner.

I decided that I wanted all of my men to stay with me in this house. Then we would not have to be separated from one another. I would take one of the rooms, and Mr. Fryer, Mr. Ledward, Mr. Nelson, and Mr. Peckover would share the other. The remaining officers would occupy the loft, while the outer apartment would provide lodging for the men. When I informed the governor of this decision, he sent chairs, tables, benches, bedding, and other items we would need.

I came to realize that the governor's illness was beyond help, that even then he was dying. So from that point on I took matters that required his assistance to his son-in-law, Mr. Timotheus Wanjon. Mr. Wanjon was actually second in authority after the governor. The earlier information I received in regard to Captain Spikerman's holding this rank was mistaken.

Mr. Wanjon was generous in sending a din-

ner to the house. My men were careful not to eat too heavily. They realized that overeating would not be good for their bodies after so long a time of near-starvation. As for me, I was less interested in food than I was in rest and quiet. In my room, however, I found that I could not rest until I had reviewed the sufferings we had endured and the thanksgiving that we owed Almighty God. There was no way we could have been able to bear our severe trials without the power He had given us.

I was especially humbled to think about how my leadership had saved eighteen lives. I had received strength to carry out my responsibility as a commander. There were constantly difficult decisions to make, and I often had to stick to those decisions in spite of tremendous pressure.

One example of this was the decision to make our food and water last as long as possible by giving out small allowances. I had to hold firmly to this plan in spite of the men's pleas to give them an increase. Perhaps you understand how difficult it is to be surrounded by people who are begging you to change your mind. And these people were weak and hungry and hurting. How easy it would have been at times to give in, but I did not do so. As a result, we had enough food and water remaining when we reached Timor that, had it been necessary, we could have gone on to Java.

Those men who were inclined to act foolishly and in haste also tested my command. As I mentioned, several of the men were eager to land at Timor as soon as we arrived there. I also would have liked to land as soon as possible, but I knew it might not be safe. The natives on this island who live at a distance from the Dutch settlement might have attacked us as those on Tofoa did. So I insisted we remain offshore until we had good reason to feel it was safe to land.

God saved us at Tofoa by causing the natives to delay their attack. We were able to cross a sea of more than twelve hundred leagues by receiving enough food and water to keep us alive. We survived storms in which the boat could easily have gone to the bottom. We could have died from disease, but were spared. We gained safe passage through islands where other unfriendly natives might have attacked us and killed us. Finally, we reached people who treated us with extreme kindness and helped us regain our health.

CHAPTER 15

Business in Coupang

T he minister's voice rang out with the familiar words of the burial service. I was listening—at least part of my mind was listening. The other part was remembering a friend. We had worked side-by-side in fulfilling our assignment. We had battled together the merciless enemy of a raging sea, and we had fought hunger and weariness and cold. But now he was dead.

I am not going to suggest that you may lose a friend to death, although that is a bitter experience that many must face. But I do want to state that we should always treat our friends as very precious persons. We never

221

know when friendships will end. They end sometimes when one friend moves far away from the other. One friend's entering into a new kind of work or into marriage or even into new religious views can mark the end of the friendship.

It puzzles me that many people treat their friends in a careless manner. They become angry with them over the smallest matters; they speak to them in an insulting way; they sometimes refuse to speak to them at all. I hope you never do such things to your friends.

What should we do with our friends? It is clear that we should love them, be patient with them, encourage them, and help them. They are with us for only a short time.

I remember that day when I stood quietly at the burial service and said a final good-bye to a friend....

As my health improved, I began to take care of other matters of business. First, I took time to prepare a formal account of how I had lost the *Bounty*. I presented this to the governor. At that same time I also asked him, in the name of his Majesty, King George the Third, for some help in possibly recovering the ship. It was my wish that he would send instructions to all Dutch settlements that if the *Bounty* appeared, they should hold it there. With this request I also included a complete description of the list of mutineers. The governor agreed to assist in this way.

Another request I made was on behalf of Mr. Nelson. I wanted our botanist to have permission to walk about the country in search of plants. It seemed likely that Timor would have some plants that might prove useful for food, medicine, or in other ways.

The governor gladly granted this request also, but it would make no difference. Mr. Nelson was seriously ill with a cold and was therefore unable to perform the task. His illness was caused in part by his failure to keep himself clothed as warmly as he should.

One additional matter of business was the purchase of a small schooner to use in sailing to Batavia. That is the Dutch capital on the island of Java. A schooner, by the way, is a large ship with two masts. The main one is in the middle of the ship, and a smaller one is nearer the bow.

I planned to sail to Batavia soon enough to be there when the October fleet made its voyage to Europe. And so I went to work fitting my thirty-four foot schooner *Resource* for the sea. Aware that the waters around Java are often visited by pirate ships, I took measures to see that the *Resource* was equipped with weapons of defense. Mr. Wanjon was kind enough to loan me four brass swivel guns, fourteen small arms, and a supply of ammunition. I promised to return these at Batavia.

On July 20, little more than one month after our arrival at Coupang, Mr. David Nelson died. His cold had grown worse, and he had suffered from a very high fever. His body was still weak from our struggles in reaching Timor, and he did not have the strength to recover.

Mr. Nelson's death was a very painful loss for me. During our difficult voyage he had shown a great deal of patience and courage. That especially meant much to me because some of the other men were putting so much pressure on me by their lack of patience and courage. Thinking back to the months spent on the *Bounty* and at Otáheite, I can say that he did an excellent job of handling the task assigned to him. It is sad, however, that all of his efforts in collecting the breadfruit plants went to waste.

The funeral took place the following day. The body of Mr. Nelson was carried by twelve soldiers dressed in black, with the minister walking ahead of them. I was next behind the soldiers, joined by Mr. Wanjon. Behind us were ten gentlemen of the town and the officers of the ships in the harbor. My officers and men were last in the procession. The body was buried behind the chapel in a burying ground used by the Europeans in the town. I regretted that I was unable to get a tombstone to place over the burial site.

One month later, August 20, we sailed from Coupang, bound for Batavia. I hardly need to speak of the affection we felt for the kind and generous people we left behind. We exchanged salutes with people at the fort and from the other ships as we moved out of the harbor. As we began this voyage, the *Resource* was towing the launch in which we had made our perilous journey from Tofoa to Coupang.

Let me tell you at this point a few facts about Coupang. Then perhaps you can have a better idea of the kind of place in which we stayed for about two months. The settlement was formed in 1630. It is the only one the Dutch have on Timor, although there are other Dutch residents elsewhere on the island. The Portuguese have a settlement on the north side of Timor. The chief products of the island are sandalwood and beeswax.

Sandalwood comes from trees that apparently grow only in this part of the world. The wood gives off a very pleasant fragrance, and that is why it is used in making perfumes. It is easily carved and serves well for making boxes, cases for holding jewelry, and walking sticks.

As the name indicates, beeswax is obtained from the honeycomb of bees. Among its uses are making candles and ointments. When the natives gather the honeycombs from the many bees on the island, they put the honey in jars. Then the wax is melted and run into blocks. These blocks are three feet long and from twelve to fifteen inches in both width and height.

The natives on the island are ruled by a king, whom the Dutch refer to as "Emperor." I was able, during my several weeks on Timor, to make a visit to the king. This elderly man welcomed me and saw that I was served refresh-

ments: tea, rice cakes, roasted Indian corn, and dried buffalo flesh. He also provided me with about a pint of arrack, a drink made from the sap of the coconut palm. Having been informed that arrack would be an acceptable present for the king, I brought some with me. When I gave it to him, he received it gladly.

The king lived in a large house. The house and the furniture were very dirty. But the king himself dressed like true royalty. His inner garment was a checked print, held in place by a silk and gold belt. Over that he wore a loose linen jacket. However, the handkerchief on his head was made of a coarse material.

The Dutch have made an effort to introduce the Christian faith to the natives. They have not met with much success, other than in the area around Coupang. The Scriptures have been translated into the Malay language used by the natives. A Malay clergyman conducts a regular service in that language in the church at Coupang.

While at Timor I learned as much as I could about the fruits grown there. As you might expect, the breadfruit was of particular interest to me. It grows in great abundance on the island, but it is not so good as that grown on Otaheite. A breadfruit of Timor weighs half as much more than one of equal size at Otaheite, but it does not have so fine a flavor. It is not used on Timor as bread, but generally eaten with milk and sugar.

When I left the governor, Mr. Van Este, he was almost at the point of death. I remember him and his son-in-law, Mr. Wanjon, with much gratitude. They extended countless benefits to me and to my men. We will never be able to repay them. I must add a word of gratitude as well for Mr. Max, the town surgeon. He ministered to our needs in a generous way. When I attempted to make arrangements to pay him, he would not accept, answering that he was merely doing his duty.

CHAPTER 16

Homeward Bound

Home—it is a wonderful word. And one's homeland is a wonderful place to see again after a long absence. When I saw England again on that long-ago day, I could hardly keep from crying. My heart swelled with joy at the familiar sights and sounds and smells of home.

Whatever your homeland is, you should appreciate it. Its language is your language, and its people are your people. Learn its history; obey its laws; honor its leaders; enjoy its benefits. And do not forget that you have a responsibility to make it a better place. The England I have known is not a perfect place, but I hope that somehow, when I am gone, I will have left it a better place.

Wherever your home is, you should appreciate it. Whether it is on a high hill or in a broad valley, along a river or near a forest, in a large city or at the edge of a small village, it is home. It is a special place, and you should always think of it in that way.

Perhaps we cannot quite appreciate our homeland and home as much as we should until we have been away from it for a long time. I had been gone for a very long time, and I had often had reason to wonder if I would ever see it again. But there it was. I was looking on it once more, and I would never forget the moment. . . .

It was on the first day of October that we reached Batavia. I wasted little time in seeing to the details involved in finding a ship to take my men and me back to England. First I paid a visit on Mr. Englehard, whose title was "the Sabandar." He was the officer through whom all strangers must take care of their business. With him I went to pay my respects to the Governor-General. When I asked permission for my men and me to board the next ship sailing for Europe, the Governor-General agreed to that. He also gave me permission to sell the schooner and the launch.

My health took a sudden turn for the worse. That night in my hotel room the air seemed much too hot for me, and I had difficulty breathing. Then I became ill with a severe headache. The next day the headache grew worse, and I also developed a very high fever.

Thinking that I might feel better away from the city, I asked Mr. Englehard to make arrangements for me to move to a house in the country. At sunrise a few days later, I left the hotel and was carried to the house of Mr. Sparling, the surgeon general. He lived about four miles from the city and near a hospital.

The cool, fresh country air did help me to feel better for a short while. However, my illness soon began to grow worse again. Mr. Sparling would not allow me to take any medicine. He felt that I needed to leave Batavia, and so he advised me to sail for England as soon as possible.

My hopes of sailing home together with my men could not be fulfilled. The Governor-General informed me that the ships leaving for Europe were all crowded. That meant my men and I would have to travel separately. I was able to arrange passage for myself and two others on a packet that was due to sail on October 16. Let me explain that a packet is a passenger boat that makes regular trips carrying mail and cargo.

On Saturday, October 10, an Englishman named Captain John Eddie purchased the *Resource* at a public sale. I was disappointed at how low the purchase price was, but there was nothing I could do about it.

On that same day the launch was sold. Perhaps you can understand that it was a

painful experience to part with it. It had served us so well during our voyage that I would have liked to have kept it. However, I had no way of transporting it to England.

Another event on that day was the death of one more companion on our perilous voyage. Thomas Hall had been ill since the time of our arrival at Timor, and once we reached Batavia, I arranged for him to be sent to the hospital. He had served on the *Bounty* as a cook. Now he became the second of our company to die since we made it to Timor.

At seven o'clock on the morning of October 16, the packet sailed from Batavia. On board along with me were the clerk, Mr. John Samuel, and a seaman, John Smith. The Governor-General had assured me that the rest of my men would follow me as soon as passage could be arranged. He would try to see that they were separated as little as possible.

Our voyage home took us to the Cape of Good Hope, where we anchored in Table Bay.

I went into Cape Town to visit Governor Vander Graaf. My purpose was to work out a problem. It seems that the Dutch East India Company has a standing order that no person who sails from Batavia to Europe on one of their ships may leave the ship before it arrives at its intended port.

If I could not get that changed, I would have to go on to Holland. Because I was eager to get home to England, I was determined to do everything I could in order to be able to leave the ship early. With the permission of the Governor-General at Batavia, I used his name in requesting that I be allowed to leave the packet while in the English Channel. This request was granted.

We proceeded through the eastern Atlantic, past the island St. Helena, past the island Ascension, and past the Cape de Verde Islands. Finally, on Sunday, March 14, 1790, I left the packet and boarded an Isle of Wight boat. Shortly afterward I landed at Ports-

mouth on England's southern coast. I had been gone for two years and three months.

As the Governor-General at Batavia had promised, my officers and men were allowed to sail on ships that departed not long after mine. However, I learned that three more of them would never come home.

When I boarded the packet in Batavia, all of the surviving men appeared to be in good health. But within two weeks of my departure Mr. Elphinstone, master's mate, and Peter Linkletter, seaman, both died. Also, during his voyage with the Dutch fleet bound for Europe, Robert Lamb died. At the time of this writing we have not heard anything about Mr. Ledward, the surgeon.

There were nineteen men forced into the launch by the mutineers. Every one of us could have perished in the sea or at the hands of natives. But it pleased God that twelve of us should survive all the difficulties and dangers of the voyage and live to see England again.

And so I have come to the end of my story. As I have told you of these events, I have tried to explain to you what you needed to know to understand what it means to be a captain at sea. You know more about ships and sailing, I hope, and about the islands and people of the South Seas.

Perhaps the best thing you can take with you is this: When you face trials, disappointments, and discouragements, do not give up. You can always find a way to endure it and to come out triumphant in the end.

Now that you have finished this book, I hope you have more questions. "What did William Bligh do after he returned to England?" "What happened to Fletcher Christian and the rest of the mutineers?" "How about the *Bounty*? Did it ever sail again?" Let me give you a few answers to such questions.

Captain William Bligh later became Governor Bligh. He went to what we now know as Australia in 1805 to govern the colony there. Remember that had begun as a colony of prisoners. Bligh's rule of this colony was not successful. He attempted to do away with the liquor trade there, and that was not a popular move. In other ways he seems to have been a poor choice for governor.

He returned to England in 1808. Three years later he received an appointment as a rear admiral in the British Navy. In 1814 he was promoted to vice admiral. But he never held an actual command during these years.

Bligh died in December of 1817, almost exactly thirty years after beginning his famous voyage on the *Bounty*. He was sixty-three years old at the time of his death.

The mutineers did return to Otaheite/Tahiti, but they did not all remain there long. In 1790 nine of them took six Tahitian men and twelve of the women in the *Bounty* to a place called Pitcairn Island. This island, discovered in 1767, is only two and one-half miles long and one mile wide. It is located about halfway between Australia and South America. No one lived there until the mutineers and their Tahitians arrived.

They destroyed the *Bounty* after reaching Pitcairn Island. (Its remains were discovered there in 1957.) Then, it seems, they destroyed one another. Only one of the mutineers, a man named John Adams, survived as late as 1808. However, descendants of Fletcher

Christian and of the other mutineers still live on the island today.

At the beginning of this book I referred to the book, *Mutiny on the Bounty*, by Charles Nordhoff and James William Hall. Let me now add that Nordhoff and Hall wrote two more books about the *Bounty*. *Men Against the Sea* tells the story of Bligh and his eighteen men in the launch. *Pitcairn Island* describes the later adventures of Christian and the other mutineers.

The famous British poet, Lord Byron, based his poem, "The Island," on the events in this book.

Let me close with one last, interesting fact: The breadfruit plan in the West Indies did not work. The slaves, it seems, preferred plaintains.